'Emma Bridgewater, queen of kitch[...]
of the memoir too. As attractive, [...]
as her products, this book is simi[...]
cloying cosiness. The crunch of go[...]
ness of good marmalade in fact.'   Stephen [...]

'Emma Bridgewater's captivating recipe for a happy family life:
food, passion, work, love.'   Meg Rosoff

'A wonderful memoir... absolutely brimming over with the
resolution to make life full and funny and beautiful and
delicious and properly engaged with all the things that matter.'
                                                  Adam Nicolson

'An enchanting insight into the story behind the much loved
Bridgewater Pottery interspersed with glimpses into the sweet-
ness of country life and the values and comforting food many
of us hold so dear.'
                          Darina Allen, Ballymaloe Cookery School

'Packed with moving vignettes... a paean to a childhood love of
adventure.'   *Harpers Bazaar*

'*Toast & Marmalade* is a heartwarming, sumptuously presented
memoir-cum-commemoration of the Emma Bridgewater brand.'
                                                   You Magazine

'It is hard not to fall for this narrator, who comes across as all
of a piece: sagacious, plain-speaking and energetic, labouring
at her pottery, her family life and the writing process, to bring
them all into something not far off perfection.'
                                            [...], World of Interiors

TOAST & MARMALADE

TOAST & MARMALADE

STORIES FROM THE KITCHEN DRESSER, A MEMOIR

First published as *Toast & Marmalade and Other Stories* in Great Britain in
2014 by Saltyard Books
An imprint of Hodder & Stoughton
An Hachette UK company

This paperback edition first published in 2015

1

ISBN 978 1 473 60431 5
EBOOK ISBN 978 1 473 61621 9

Typeset in Plantin Light by Palimpsest Book Production Ltd,
Falkirk, Stirlingshire

Copy editor Bryony Nowell
Proofreader Annie Lee

Printed and bound by Clays Ltd, St Ives plc

Hodder & Stoughton policy is to use papers that are natural, renewable and
recyclable products and made from wood grown in sustainable forests. The
logging and manufacturing processes are expected to conform to the
environmental regulations of the country of origin.

Saltyard Books
338 Euston Road
London NW1 3BH

www.saltyardbooks.co.uk

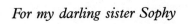

For my darling sister Sophy

CONTENTS

* * *

These are just stories   I

Toast and marmalade   5

Spongeware shards and dreaming up
  my own shapes   15

Making it real   27

Camping, surfing and swimming
  underwater   39

An office in Chelsea   51

We lived on Love Street   59

Thousands of miles and too much
  country music   69

To the memory of Charlotte   85

Little altars everywhere   95

Matthew knows a lot about chickens   107

A jar of mustard and a box of matches   117

Friday night at Minety 129

The Raggle Taggle Gypsies-O 137

Life is a patchwork quilt 145

No more directors' dining rooms
in the Potteries 155

Print, pattern and lots of bright
colours 165

Stalking figs 175

Votes for women 183

Kelburn Granny's china shoes 199

My, but Miss Meakin, you're beautiful 207

What is it about kitchen dressers? 219

Acknowledgements 227

* * *

THESE ARE JUST
STORIES

STORIES about people, places, events and encounters – stories woven into narratives over the years to explain and remember some of the important and pivotal feelings; the moments when the game changed. To anyone I have included, and to those numerous people I have left out, these stories may sound odd, even unrecognisable; to them I bow, and beg that they understand and show forbearance, for as I say, these are only stories.

And I am, as the book goes to print, overwhelmed by flocks more stories; they dangle amongst the Christmas decorations in shop windows, wait amongst the pillows when I go to bed, slip out from between the pages of books on the shelves as I pass, rattle amongst the teacups and rustle in the curtains – all the stories I didn't tell.

When I am asked about the slightly unlikely course of my career – after school and university experiences which yielded no clues to indicate that I would spend my working life in manufacturing, or design, or business – the chapters that follow are some of the explanations that I proffer.

Instead of smooth sailing on a sunny day, as I picture other people going about their working lives, it seems as if I have been frantically trying to learn to sail a boat that I built in my sleep, then in a moment of delirium boarded and set out on a round-the-world trip – with no map, or oilskins, or even much of a picnic.

I set out to make everyday pottery in 1984; it startles me to realise that that is nearly 30 years ago, as it feels so much longer. And of course it would have been disastrous, a complete shipwreck, if not for the support, intervention and sheer hard work of an enormous number of people, who in various metaphorical roles as stern coastguards, plucky lifeboat men, tireless oarsmen, experienced pilots, cheerful crew members and cheering fellow travellers have kept the ship afloat, and made the company what it is today. Some of these people you will meet in the pages of this book; others remain in the backstory, invisible but nonetheless important.

You can either sit down and read this book from cover to cover, or dip in and out of it, piecing the stories together to experience the whole as a patchwork quilt, which is how I like it best.

TOAST AND MARMALADE

G OD, I'M GREEDY. I think about some sorts of
food a lot. Bacon, for example. Over the years I
have developed a promiscuous butcher's habit in my
fidgety desire to find streaky bacon smoked just right,
sliced thin enough and, most importantly, with just the
right amount of fat, which is more than the current
thinking tends to dictate – but as only the people who
really love their food know, it's the fat which makes
bacon taste truly delicious. In Norfolk my favourite
butcher, after extensive research, was Crawford at
Whites in Aylsham. And sometimes the sweet family
who together run Rutlands in Melton Constable. In
Oxford I favour Feller's in the Covered Market, where

I commend to you the handsome, helpful tall guy. But you must ask very nicely to get your order sliced especially thin, and be happy to come back later as it takes a bit of time. Pancetta affumicata, from an Italian deli, can make a delicious alternative. No fuss there about slicing thinly.

And when you get your bacon home, you have to cook it in a roasting pan inside the oven; never fry it. Or not indoors anyway. And it must be cooked exactly to the very perfect point. I know I'm not alone in this, and I often watch the people ahead of me in the breakfast queue in a service station at seven in the morning – they are every bit as keen as I am not to get the pink floppy undercooked bacon. They want to choose exactly those crispy, delicious slices.

My first grown-up ally in greed in many aspects, especially including breakfast, was an actor called Ken Cranham, who often came to stay at weekends in Rawlinson Road. Mum adored Ken. She said she loved all sorts of things about him, for example his habit of ringing her up at odd moments to say that he dreamed about her last night – maybe picturing her big brown mannish hands kneading the bread – then ringing off when the pips went, saying *Love you* just as the 2p ran out. She especially liked a short telephone conversation.

And she loved that Ken was greedy; she said it was a good sign in a person, and it made cooking the endless procession of meals so much more fun when someone enjoyed them as much as he did. As I write this, in a café in Norfolk 35 years on, I can vividly picture a typical Sunday morning scene in her Oxford kitchen: my brother Tom is eating a small mixing bowlful of Shreddies with brown sugar and milk, in the crumby spot where my little sisters, Nell and Clover, had toast fingers and boiled eggs earlier. My stepfather, Rick, is wheedling me –

Oh go on Em, make me some more fried eggs, and a bit of toast, and ketchup, yum.

Mum is drinking milky coffee and yawning rather a lot. Drawn by the smell of Rick's huge fry-up, Ken comes in, leaving his current glamorous girlfriend upstairs, having promised to bring her tea. He is making a beeline for the bread, which has just come out of the oven, cuts some rather fragile slices and ferries them to the grill.

Char (it sounds Shar), *your bread is amazing, but toasted, it is even better,* he sighs.

I offer to watch it for him, so he carefully chooses a plate from the pile on the dresser and a knife from the drawer underneath, and fussocks about looking for marmalade. It is in a huge brown stoneware pot, so he doesn't immediately spot it. Mum has just been making large quantities of deep, dark gold marmalade, as she does every February, using as little sugar as possible plus a few spoonfuls of black treacle, and between us we eat so much in a year that she doesn't usually have enough jam jars, so she also fills other more eccentric containers, such as this.

When the toast is ready, Ken butters it lavishly and spoons on as much marmalade as he can fit onto each mouthful. It's impossible not to want the same, so I make more toast, and more again. The combination of new brown bread, toasted, still warm, with the melting butter mixing into the golden-brown syrupy marmalade with its big, rough chunks of orange peel, is unbeatably delicious. This morning, bacon would be one step too far, we agree, and I put the last slice of the first loaf under the grill.

Rick has finished his second plate of eggs, and turns to Tom,

Tomsie, will you go to South Parade and get the papers? Oh dooo... Mum interrupts, saying,

Oh Rick, stop fagging everyone, get dressed and walk down there. You will feel much better for it. And don't eat another egg. You will get fat.

Tom slips out of the kitchen saying he's going to see Charlie, his friend who lives over the road. Mum announces that she's going to get dressed and asks,

Will you come to church with me and the babies, darling? The service is at Phil & Jim at 11.

Rick wanders off to change out of Mum's dressing gown into jeans, murmuring about being bullied. Ken wipes his face on a tea towel and takes two cups of tea back to bed. I do a bit of rudimentary wiping and piling up of plates, then check the larder for flour, butter, sugar and golden syrup, planning to make a steamed treacle pudding to have after the roast lamb at lunch. Then my cousin Kate comes shyly into the kitchen. I'd forgotten about her during the toast-frenzy, but am happy that she is in time to stop me eating a third slice. She stayed last night following a beery rugby club dance in a pavilion somewhere down the Botley Road. We settle into a post-mortem of who snogged whom, and who wept in the loos, until Mum comes and chivvies me into action.

Returning home from St Philip & St James' an hour later with Nell & Clover both sleeping in their huge pram, a waft of incense and the delicious sense of having done the right thing haloing Mum's shaggy (probably teddy bear) fur coat, we find Rick reading the papers and sitting on the ones he hasn't read yet. Kate is scrubbing potatoes in the scullery sink with Ken's girlfriend. Maybe she was called Viv? There were several of them: all beautiful; often kind to teenage girls; always actresses, sometimes quite well-known ones. Ken has walked down to the Anchor to buy cigarettes for Rick.

I'm sure lunch was delicious, and afterwards we probably walked across a wintery Port Meadow to Binsey, with the babies in the pram again, and Tom and Charlie buzzing around us on bikes. Maybe we went as far as the treacle well beside the little church across the Thames and made wishes. On the way home perhaps we picked a big bunch of twigs from the balsam poplars by the river, to put in a jug in the hall so that the heat indoors would unfurl the strange- and lovely-smelling leaves ahead of spring. Then back to Rawlinson Road again with, for me, a sinking feeling about homework not yet done, but the prospect of tea and maybe crumpets to keep my spirits up.

Mum and Rick moved from Oxford to a village called Minety, in Wiltshire, in 1980, at around the time I left home to go to university. I loved the kitchen in the new house, but I was always going back to Rawlinson Road in my mind.

I was looking for a birthday present for Mum one day, about four years on from that date. I wanted to give her something personal, and something that showed her that I wanted to be with her, even though I was not there much at the time. I decided that a pair of cups and saucers would be just the thing, conjuring up the image of us sitting together talking, drinking coffee, eating toast and, maybe, honey.

I went to one of those old-fashioned china shops that there used to be lots of, in search of cosy shapes and colourful patterns, with Mum's kitchen in mind. What I found were indeed lots of cups and saucers: mostly in the Botanic Garden pattern by Portmeirion, which I thought angular and heavy; or Denby, which was much too dull; or white and gold formal nonsense; or even figurines (help!) from Doulton; or incomprehensible, biscuity, pale blue Wedgwood with sprigged classical motifs. But none of the china for sale bore any relation to the feeling of Mum's kitchen. As I surveyed the shelves, with their internal lighting and insistence on formality and orderliness, I realised that this was all completely out of step with the way she lived: her big chipped painted dresser – in Wiltshire as in Oxford – was covered in messy, relaxed kit for a non-matching sort of life. Every day she mixed old things from markets, or china out of Granny's cupboards, with things bought on holiday abroad, big chipped Deruta mugs, Mason's Brown Quails and plates from Habitat with pink rims.

Where was the easy-going everyday china – colourful, relaxed, fun to use?

Suddenly I could see it, on my mind's dresser. I knew what it looked like, and I knew that I wanted to make it. For several months (or perhaps ever since I had started to worry about a career, at about 15) I had been searching

11

for an idea for a product or service that I could really put my heart into, to build a worthwhile company.

This was it! Hooray! I felt ecstatic. Luckily I had not the faintest idea of what lay ahead.

BROWN BREAD

* * *

Makes three 1kg loaves

Tip 1.5kg spelt flour (white or wholegrain, the choice is yours) into a very large, warm bowl. Stir in 2 sachets (4 teaspoons) of easy-blend fast action yeast and 1 tablespoon of salt. Pour in 900ml warm water (approximately 30°C) and, using your right hand only, stir and amalgamate the flour mixture with the water. Though it may get messy, do persevere – the dough will soon come together. Work the dough into a ball, then knead for a few minutes, still using only your right hand (I turn the bowl anti-clockwise with my left hand as I do this). Cover with a clean tea towel and leave on the side in a warm kitchen to double in size. This should take 3–4 hours. Turn the dough out onto a lightly-floured surface and knead again for a few minutes until smooth, knocking the dough back to its original mass. Divide into three. Knead each piece into a neat shape and put it into a greased 1kg loaf tin. Leave somewhere warm again until the loaves have doubled in size. Preheat the oven to 190°C/170°C fan/gas 5. Bake for 35 minutes, then remove the loaves from their tins and return to the oven for another 10–15 minutes. They are done when they sound hollow when tapped on the base. Leave to cool on a wire rack before slicing. This makes the most heavenly toast – you will never look back.

SPONGEWARE SHARDS AND
DREAMING UP MY OWN SHAPES

BEACHCOMBING in London sounded exciting when I first heard about it from my boyfriend Alex and his brother Anthony (in the early 1980s). Now it seems positively exotic, as pretty much every jetty, pontoon or gate that gives onto the Thames in London is festooned with razor wire, making it almost impossible to get down to the beaches which are uncovered along the river at low tide. Maybe this is as well, as the river flows very strongly with ferocious swirling tides, and if you hang over the parapets and look down at the water as the tide comes in, it looks easily possible that you could find yourself cut off on one of those dirty beaches, without a way up the slimy green walls of the

Embankment. But Alex and Anthony were undeterred and probably shinned over the barriers unconcerned anyway to go mudlarking. And the result was that many of the mantelpieces, windowsills and shelves in their house in Brixton were littered with a bewitching collection of shards of broken pottery, collected along the foreshore in London.

These were varied, with plenty of ubiquitous Willow pattern and lots of serviceable brown and cream fragments from bottles and jars – beer, lemonade, cream, marmalade, facecream, toothpaste. . . all these commodities and many more used to be sold in sturdy stoneware containers which often show snatches of enthusiastic marketing ('finest available') in elegant decorative scripts. On Port Meadow in Oxford, the council are stuck in an intermittent struggle with 'bottlediggers' who arrive after dark (or anyway, when the coast is clear), raise an area of turf and scuffle about in the shallow grave of the city's municipal Edwardian rubbish. My children found this absolutely irresistible for a while and we too acquired our own grimy museum. But amongst the shards in Alex's kitchen there were lots of cheerful, brightly-coloured pieces, whose designs were clearly applied by hand and often with a happy disregard for neatness, as the motifs were frequently smudged or crooked. What was this curious, attractive and faintly familiar pottery? What had these pieces been when whole?

As proto-engineers, men prone to messy practical projects such as disembowelling motorbikes in the bathroom or deciding to rewire the top floor of the house after supper, Alex and Anthony of course knew all about this stuff. Anthony gave me a comprehensive tutorial on the subject. It turned out that much of his collection was in the Victoria and Albert Museum, and he knew this obscure subject intimately. He explained that these were pieces of domestic china – mostly bowls, with some mugs and plates – and that the ware was often stained brown not, as I assumed, from lying in the mud, but from a lifetime on the back of the kitchen range or in a slow oven. This was the broken pottery from the kitchens of the most modest houses in the city. The ware was often chipped under the glaze, indicating that it had been bought as a reject, very cheaply, perhaps from a small factory, or even scavenged from the heap to be found at the back door of every pottery works. He guessed that the decoration was sometimes done by unskilled labour, perhaps not unusually by children, and after glazing and another firing, the cheaply-priced result would have been sold on market stalls to housewives with no extra to spend on fancy china.

He said that the decorations were applied using the cut root of a natural sponge, dipped in ceramic colour and dabbed onto the ware to form simple repeat patterns. A bit like potato-printing. (I learned subsequently that

17

Irish spongeware-type pottery really was printed using a spud.) Anthony reckoned that the technique was initially a Scottish speciality, but that once it had gained some popularity, the more go-ahead Staffordshire potters got in on the act and made spongeware commercially, probably well into the twentieth century. Where could I go to look at whole pieces?

Ah. He was enigmatic about this. It was hard. This was ware that was never looked after carefully or kept for best, and as such it was well beneath the radar of museum curators, so rather difficult to say. . .

✻

I had just spent 18 months, since I left university, working for two clever, funny girls whose knitwear designs were proving popular. In my final months for Sal and Jo I recruited something like 800 knitters to make up the orders for their designs for one season, to meet fashion deadlines. It was an amazing experience, but not a situation I'd willingly re-create, I vowed. I wanted to get my designs made in a factory. Because that sounded to me like an orderly procedure. Where was I to find that factory? And how did I convert my ideas into pottery I could hold in my hand?

I turned to my most practical and gainfully employed friend. Terry was a graphic designer who I had known for some time. He had kindly put bits of work my way when I was short of money, or when he needed a simple but long job done in a hurry. I especially remember a stressful day when he asked me to write more than 250 captions for a catalogue for a sale of assorted needle-work. All the lots had previous descriptions but spread across several different brochures. I had only to find them, then re-draft them where necessary to make the various pieces sound as, well, exciting as possible, with the correct new lot numbers attached, while working from stamp-sized grey photographs. And it had to be done in a day for immediate emergency delivery to the printer, with no time for proofing as the sale was imminent. Terry knew what he was about. When I drank a cup of coffee with him in the morning before I started, I was a rank amateur at adult life who had yet to hand in so much as an essay on time; by lunchtime (a cigarette only – no time at all to eat) I was a desperate woman; and by nine that evening, when I slapped the completed catalogue on his desk, I was a grown-up. And in need of a drink. So he was a likely and, as it turned out, an inspired person to turn to with these burning questions.

One night in the autumn of 1984 when Alex and I were at a very noisy party, I found that I was experiencing a new sensation. I wanted to move away from the music and no, I didn't want to dance – I really wanted to talk about work. Terry was patient, and he also had the vital information that Stoke-on-Trent was where I was going next.

He had recently done a big job for one of the breweries. A small part of the new look for which they were paying him eye-watering sums of money was new kit for the bars of their pubs, such as water jugs, ashtrays and, most importantly, pump pulls – as ornate and elaborate as possible, fit for the chapped pink paws of the blowsiest of Sickert's barmaids. He said that Sam Spencer was the man, the best in the business of ceramic model making, and he would get me his number tomorrow – no! Wait a minute, here it was in his pocket, and yes, I wrote the number down on a fag packet on the spot. Terry said,

Call him tomorrow. Don't hang about. And when you have been to Stoke, come and tell me all about it.

The thing was, I didn't know the first thing about how to make pottery. So I made it up as I went along. But from the very beginning it never crossed my mind to use existing shapes. I pictured a little gang of my own pieces, all clearly meant for each other. From Terry I had the name and number of the model maker, someone who would actually create these pieces, so now as a matter of urgency I had to be able to describe these shapes. Just as I was sure that the shapes must be my own, and friendly to each other, so I was also sure that even if they drew their strengths from real pieces, they must be created from scratch – no copies.

My ideas about shape were – still are – based on a deep love of the look of what I understood to be English, and probably specifically Staffordshire, earthenware. In fact I now know that some of my favourite things were made in Scotland, where the east coast potteries at Kirkcaldy and Portobello were very important, as they made lots of lively spongeware; or in Sunderland, with its lustre and its engraved designs commemorating ship launches, political campaigns and, frequently, the engineering triumph of the Iron Bridge in Coalbrookdale, Shropshire.

And in truth I love lots of continental wares: such as French earthenware from Lunéville, Quimper, delftware from the Netherlands, and stencilled and aerographed nineteenth- and early-twentieth-century pieces from Villeroy & Boch. And I'm not really that committed to earthenware, as I especially like French catering porcelain such as Pillivuyt. And yet in my mind there was a shadowy but sinewy conviction about the vital importance riding on getting each shape exactly right, and I knew that I could do this. And that English earthenware would be the touchstone. This unlikely self-belief came both directly from Mum's expectations that we would be competent and practical, and at the same time from a desire to scotch her exasperating casual scepticism. When she heard what I was up to (I had to explain a bit, because she caught me red-handed loading two boxes of china into Alex's car, otherwise I'd have instinctively hidden my project from her at this tender stage), she merely said,

I think you may have to find someone who knows what they are talking about.

Then she went to commune with Bob, who helped in the garden, about sweet williams in the border along the churchyard wall, ignoring the telephone ringing in the house behind us.

✳

I had a date a few days hence with Terry's model maker, so I had to pull these ideas out of the shadows. Now.

I had decided to round up all my favourite things and assemble them in an empty upstairs room in Alex's house in Brixton, where they were watched over by a group of forlorn rusty radiators, the sort of thing that the brothers could never leave in a skip. Like Beatrix Potter's Mr Tod, I had more than one home and, also like him, I had no qualms about borrowing from the kitchen china in all of them. My other bolt-hole, when life in Brixton was unappealing, was my cousin Desmond's house in Chelsea, where the china was of a much more useful and serviceable character than the facilities (including the hot water geyser, which banged and wheezed and created maximum suspense before igniting with a whoosh to produce a frugal hot water supply), or the heating – there wasn't any. But the china was lavish and varied, and in its ranks I found inspirational dishes and bowls.

Alex and Anthony had lots of nice pottery and this too I herded upstairs, selectively.

When I had about 40 or 50 pieces, I corralled them into groups, their personalities becoming clearer as I sorted them by type. I lay on the floor among them and thought about the things I wanted to create. Alex had already, in characteristically practical and slightly roundabout fashion, found a woodturner to make a wooden mug. It had – still has – a ridged foot, in imitation of the basic technique of mug-making in nineteenth-century potteries, namely putting the thrown mug onto a lathe to turn a crisply defined foot, like the base of a column. The handle would be added at the end. Following this tradition, I Sellotaped a handle made of thin card onto the wooden mug. If I narrowed my eyes, I could believe it was real and complete.

This mug was the centrepiece. I was well aware that I was likely to sell more mugs than anything else and this was to be the definitive mug, full of conviction – cosy, commanding, right. But I had no interest in just selling a collection of mug designs. Instead I had a picture in my mind, fixed since that day a few weeks previously, of the dresser of colourful pottery, worthy of Mum's kitchen, filled with my wares. I needed plates, bowls, jugs, and a serving plate or a big bowl for drama in the display. I ranged mentally among the pots on the floor around me, thinking about kitchens. I could not afford to make more than four or five shapes to begin with, so each one had to be telling.

And in due course I drew a simple milk jug shape in which I hoped to encapsulate all the bustling, practical, pleasing characteristics of the best jug. And I found a small, straight-sided bowl, which I redrew as a little bigger and fatter than its Scottish original. This was the right bowl for the right food: yoghurt and honey; lentil soup; apple crumble and custard – this was to be the bowl you would search for before ever wielding a spoon again. That settled, I turned my mind to a serving dish, a decent-sized item and preferably one that would fit on the shelves of most dressers. I remembered a lovely deep blue plate, made as a christening present for one of my sisters, about 10 inches in diameter and about 2 inches deep, which was always on the top shelf of Mum's dresser. I had not had the courage to borrow that, but no matter, it was in my mind. And here was another, this one from Desmond's kitchen, slightly deeper with a steeper profile. What was the perfect dish to serve a tomato salad? Or mashed potatoes, or a risotto, or egg mayonnaise? Or, for that matter, to put on the windowsill full of ripe plums? Or in the hall, for car keys and parking money? I drew a generous, round, shallow bowl, then went downstairs to measure shelf heights in Alex's kitchen. Lastly I considered plate sizes and profiles, and when I was clear about this, I put the drawings together in a sketchbook and felt equipped.

Now – fired up by Alex's broken china and the vision of making a range of contemporary earthenware to suit my mother's idiosyncratically informal kitchen, with the shapes drawn and experiments in decoration under way in the Brixton kitchen – I was in the grip of A Vision. Now I could almost perfectly see my dresser covered in new spongeware pottery. It was lovely. I really liked it. And I was quite sure that others would too. But how on earth did I get this pottery made? How to sell it? A lot of questions crowded my mind.

I date from exactly this time the dreadful one-track minded nature of my relationship with my business. I became, almost overnight it seemed, a crazed obsessive, condemned (I suppose voluntarily, but it didn't feel like it) to bend the ear of all comers, late into the night, long after the subject should have been changed, ages after bedtime – I was unable to let the subject drop. I became the Ancient Mariner of the Potteries, and I here apologise unreservedly to everyone who has been on the receiving end. All the more so because I can't

25

promise that it's over. The fever has subsided but I get recurrent outbreaks. Anything can trigger an attack. It's probably with me for life.

MAKING IT REAL

SAM WIGGLED his eyebrows. I felt acutely anxious. I had taken enormous care over each curve and every measurement; I needed to communicate exactly what I wanted the pots to look like, but it seemed inevitable that my amateur drawings were completely hopeless. I wriggled uncomfortably on the very dusty chair in Sam's rather bleak office. He had spread my drawings, and the life-sized silhouettes that I had carefully mounted on black paper, all over his dusty desk, his very dusty photocopier and the dusty filing cabinets.

It had been a brisk, sunny morning when I left London, but was raining when the train drew into Stoke-on-Trent.

Outside the dirty windows now, the autumn day seemed to be getting dark, though it was just after midday.

Oh heavens, I'm so sorry. My drawings – are they no good? I'm afraid it's my first attempt. Tell me what else?

I floundered and stammered to a halt. Sam smiled, wiggled his eyebrows some more and said,

No, no. The drawings are ok. It's like the old days. In fact you are a bit of an old-fashioned girl, aren't you?

I relaxed, and realised on the spot that it was going to be all right: he wasn't going to chuck me out and tell me I was wasting his time. In fact the reverse, as he leapt nimbly to his feet (I noticed that, whilst dusty, his shoes were very shiny) and his white overall rustled with keenness.

Let's go down to the workshop and I'll show you how it's done.

I followed him down the rickety stairs. The offices, loo and kitchen were slung above the loading bay at the front of his building, whilst the pottery making was at the back. As we walked through the factory, Sam said,

I'll give you a look at the making process afterwards, if you are interested, but let's start with the modelling, eh?

Everyone in the place wore the same white overalls, and now I could see why. What I had taken for household dust in the office, assuming that housework wasn't his

thing, was of course clay dust. It gave the whole long room a ghostly look, as everything, especially the hair and eyebrows of the people working there, was thickly coated with it. The overalls were strictly practical, intended to keep your clothes clean. But, to my untrained eye, the workers all had the look of dental assistants with very grey hair, though that might have been heightened by the latex gloves which some of the girls wore, and which I found a tiny bit spooky. Sam looked more like a school dinner lady but perhaps the clay dust was saying 'flour' to me. Anyway, I felt excited, if confused, and followed him eagerly.

Along one side of the factory, to take advantage of the windows (though the view was of a bank overgrown with brambles in which plastic bags flapped amongst the fag packets and newspapers), Sam had partitioned off a slice of the room to make a modelling workshop.

There was a desk, a wheel, a lathe and some shelves stacked with clumsy-looking white shapes of all sorts and sizes – cubes, cylinders, slices, wedges and many more. On the desk were callipers, files, knives, rulers, set squares, pencils and piles and piles of papers.

Right. So. This is how we make a mug.

Sam pulled out my drawings and began to explain. He would make a rough, solid cylinder out of plaster of

Paris, larger than the body of my mug. For the moment we would forget about the handle – that would be modelled separately. He would set that block on the lathe, fixing it in a clamp. Leaving a base for the clamp to hold onto, he would spin the block and slowly carve away the plaster, leaving sufficient to allow for the foot of the mug. And he would continue carving until he revealed the mug. I nodded, but felt foggy.

Sensing this, he got down from the shelves other shapes of handleless jugs, cups and mugs. They were pure white, a bit like finished bone china, but solid, not hollowed out. Their handles were held on with Blu-Tack. He put a model beside its finished child – a decorated piece of cream pottery – explaining that the model (positive) is used to make a block (negative), from which you cast a case (positive), from which you make working moulds (negative) for the factory to use. The moulds were the clumpy shapes I had first noticed. A mug mould looks like a grooved white Cheddar cheese, hollowed out, which comes apart in three pieces.

He shook my drawing and said,

Now, some questions. First, which side is the right height? Joking. They are very close. Do you want a soft or a crisp finish to the detailing on the foot? And is there any detail on the handle?

And we were off. He was taking this seriously. We went through the four shapes, with queries and explanations, and Sam assured me that the finished articles would indeed look very like my drawings. He would make a rough model of all four pieces, and I was to come back in a week to confirm each one before he went to block stage.

✳

So, do you want to see the making now?

You bet I did. He walked me through the factory stages, first showing me the trows, which are long slatted tables (one for each caster) where the moulds are lined up, all held together with elastics. The moulds are filled with liquid clay, then left to stand for the mysterious 'right' length of time to create the perfect weight of pot; then they are tipped to pour out excess slip, leaving a skin of clay lining the inside of the mould, and left to stand again; finally the mould is cracked, revealing the piece in a fragile state, with seams showing the lines of the mould.

In the next department, just the other side of some trolleys loaded with drying wares, one very resilient lady, who spends the whole day with her hands plunged in and out of cold water, smoothes or fettles the seams away using a knife and a sponge. Sam explained that if the ware is destined for a printed (or litho) decoration, it is biscuit-fired after fettling, glazed, fired again, then the decoration is applied onto the glaze, after which it receives a third firing.

Under some strip lights I watched as two ladies chatted, deftly sticking on transfer-printed decorations of brewer's logos and slogans. The radio blared, while Cliff Richard pranced and grinned above the radiator on a page torn out of a magazine. They stopped talking while I stood and watched. Sam started to ask about decoration for my wares and I did not immediately reply, as I was interested to see how long they spent decorating each piece.

Those transfers will have to be fired again to fuse them into the glaze, Sam pointed out.

I later learned that Sam's factory is a useful example of a very typical way to make and decorate pottery, developed in this part of Staffordshire during the Industrial Revolution by farmers as a seasonal variant on farming, providing them with some extra income in winter. He said that the number, temperature and sequence of the firings varied depending on the effects sought in the different factories, each of which had tended over the years to evolve its own look and technique. But this whole process, exactly as achieved in Sam's factory, would be completely familiar to a potter from 1780. Our set-up in 2014 is essentially timeless; this is the traditional Staffordshire way of making domestic crockery.

*

Meeting over, Sam called through into the next-door office and asked his wife to phone for a taxi for me. I had a good quarter of an hour to wait before the rattling Datsun arrived, and I walked up and down in the drizzle. Sam's neighbours drove white vans and large German saloons. I thought this looked prosperous but I was to learn that, as a rough guide, the bigger the car outside a backstreet business, the shakier the concern, as the receiver lets you keep a car if your business goes into liquidation. It didn't look as if the neighbours would be very particular about what they poured down the drains. The signboards were anonymous: Zoom, Tony Designs, Dez Ltd. These various businesses were all housed in prefab or breezeblock sheds of varying sizes. Litter blew down the road like tumbleweed in Tombstone, despite the wet. And the road was more of a lane – the potholes joined up in places – and it straggled along a scrap of land squeezed between a railway and a recently built dual carriageway. About 300 yards from Sam's there was a triangle of grass with a row of cottages, about half of which were boarded up. The grass ended in chain-link fence, and the lorries roared past behind an embankment just beyond it. Three boys were riding their bikes on the grass – they had made a ramp with some blocks and planks – and two goats were tethered on one corner of the green, beside a chip van which was just finishing its midday shift. As I looked I realised that this was the remnant of a village, the rest of which must lie under the dual carriageway. I felt a pang of melancholy, which was dispelled by the arrival of my cheerful taxi driver in his amazingly smelly taxi. I departed for the station, where I got out, feeling hungry and fiercely dehydrated.

✳

When I returned a week later, Sam had made my drawings real. I could see that we needed to effect some changes. For example we fiddled with the jug, because in real clay my curves were too swooping; the profile needed simplification. This was easily achieved as Sam scraped carefully at the plaster model while it spun on his lathe, so that its bosom became less buxom – a little bit of weight loss, basically. Then we set the plaster mug and jug side by side, held the card handles cut from my drawings against them and squinted assessingly.

I had made both handles too swingy – the jug would be unwieldy to pour, and both shapes a bit awkward to lift and hold – so we re-drew them to sit closer to the body and squinted some more until they were right. The bowl was simple: it came right first time, as did the dish, though being wide and shallow it was impossible to judge unless you stooped right down until your eye was at table level.

When I left this time, we agreed that Sam would

need a couple of weeks to take all four pieces to block stage, then cast two of each, so I could see what they would really, truly look like. I could hardly curb my excitement, but left in the knowledge that I needed to get to work on the spongeware patterns, bearing in mind that Sam's decorating ladies, whose names I knew to be Anne and Marie, seemed to spend about 90 seconds on a large pub ashtray. I was intrigued to see if I could make my patterns take something like this amount of a decorator's time, as I was hoping to keep the costs as low as possible.

This visit also included a more detailed conversation with Sam about my plans. We had priced the modelling, which seemed like much the most exciting £450 I could possibly imagine spending. And we had agreed that if all went well, I would buy 100 of each piece to take away to use for my decorating experiments. My cousin Kate and I were working to keep body and soul together (just) by making canapés for drinks parties. I'd have to put in lots of extra days over the next few weeks.

Alex's house was partly civilised, with a nice, peaceful, quite empty drawing room with rather grown-up curtains and sometimes a fire in the fireplace; and it was partly feral, with nothing but piles of skip-finds in several rooms. There was a solitary loo, which was in an outhouse in the garden (less feral than old-fashioned, but undeniably cold in winter), and punk lodgers who came and went at all hours. I adored one of these, Jill, but never got over feeling shy around her wild boyfriend Tom, after the time when I found him unconscious the morning after a fancy dress party, for which Jill had covered him in baked beans and wrapped him in cling film. I hadn't seen them go out and I thought he'd been mugged as he lay on the floor in the gory remains of his costume. Plus, Jill's Staffy was vigilant in his guard dog duties, so sometimes getting into the house was nerve-racking.

The bathroom was on the ground floor. It had a large cast-iron bath, a big basin and a shower fitted into the chimney-breast, so sometimes clumps of soot dropped on you while you washed. And it served as the passage through to a photographic dark room. This could lead to unexpected interruptions during peaceful reading in the bath. But there was plenty of room for a kiln, Alex was sure of this.

He and I had disagreed early on about the business: he wanted to set up a craft pottery in south London while I was convinced that I would work with a factory. The tussle was conducted slowly and fairly peacefully, as he had a lot of work on. But this was the fault line in our relationship, which would eventually open up into a gulf. In the meantime he was involved in the project, between photography jobs, and together we made frequent trips to Potterycrafts in Battersea to buy brushes, palette knives, underglaze colours and glaze.

Sam was as good as his word, and I went to collect 100 pieces of each shape. They had been fired to make them stronger, but not to full temperature, so they were still absorbent, which Sam had thought would be best when I had described to him our plans for hand-printing patterns with a sponge.

So the patterns were the next challenge. But it seemed clumsy to try to get the pieces back to Stoke again after decorating them, in order to be glazed and fired. Alex was wonderfully confident that we could learn to glaze our wares, then stack them into a small kiln (no bigger than a domestic cooker as it turned out) and fire them ourselves.

Hey presto.

I am perfectly certain that I would not have managed to glaze and fire the ware without him, but it was right up his street. After a session under instruction from Sam's dipper in Chemical Lane, some off-hand clues from Potterycrafts staff – and after a couple of disasters before we understood about wiping the glaze extra carefully off the base of the ware that touched the kiln shelves – we did it!

For two or three months at the start of 1985, with

Alex's on and off involvement, I worked on patterns, putting the winners aside and scurrying to the Jubilee Market at Covent Garden on Sundays to raise some urgent funds by selling the samples I didn't need to keep.

This was very clearly a transitional period in my mind; I had no interest in doing any part of the making process for a moment longer than I had to. The focus was on developing a sample collection to show to shops. The ware for the orders, when the orders came, as I was sure they would, must be made in a factory such as Sam's.

CAMPING, SURFING AND SWIMMING UNDERWATER

TENTS SMELL LOVELY, don't they? Slightly musty, a whiff of grass, something they finish the canvas with, socks – holidays. Some of my earliest, best images of my father from my childhood are about tents, and camping in the summer orchard. He made up his camp bed in the nice white canvas tent from his own childhood, which had been extraordinarily well looked after, and he used sheets and blankets. He taught us to cook a proper breakfast with bacon, sausages, eggs fried neatly and toast which wasn't all blackened, the whole operation done on a proper fire, which he showed us exactly how to make. All of these skills often came in very handy ever afterwards.

And after our camp breakfast, Tom, Sophy and I would spend hours and hours in the swimming pool, which Pop had made on the edge of the orchard, where it met the lawn. We had been sad to discover, on a weekend earlier in the year, that to make way for the pool, the builders had pulled down the apple tree with the robin's nest. But we really loved the pool, and so forgot the robin and learned to dive, then to do back dives, and handstands under water, and handstands off the edge into the water. By the end of the first swimming-pool summer, Tom could swim three lengths under water, whereas I couldn't quite manage to finish that third length. And for Soph it was a godsend: all those days in the pool meant that she learned to swim like a seal.

When the holidays were over, we took the camping craze back to Oxford and put up our tents in the wild back garden, beyond the screen of gooseberry bushes, nicely out of sight of the kitchen window. The Hewitt children from next door, or some of them at least, and Choss from number four and Charlie from opposite all brought their tents and camped with us, because Mum didn't mind about her flower beds – didn't even own a mower yet – and tacitly it was understood that there was more licence allowable from our mother than from theirs. So we played dares and kiss chase, and cooked suppers and breakfasts on a fire, and clambered over the garden walls and trespassed in all the neighbouring gardens.

Over the following summers we had a deal with Mum that if we wanted to sleep in the garden during term time, it was to be on Friday and Saturday nights only, and between April and October. This was decided after she came out to kiss us one night and found our hair frosted to the grass. In due course we dispensed with tents, instead making a huge bed out of old carpets that we dragged out of the shed, and making a top layer of coats to keep off the rain. Meanwhile, large numbers of people came and went inside the house, for lunch, or supper or staying the night, and while we camped out under the stars, the sounds of one long party streamed distantly out of the kitchen windows.

Tom is three years younger than me, with Sophy in the middle. As I watch Michael and Margaret camping and picnicking I can see many echoes of our childhood.

Matthew and I have been lazy about it recently, but before Margaret and Mikey were born we did some very energetic camping. In the early days of living in Norfolk, while we were still in the rented farmhouse in Worstead, I bought a ten foot square white canvas tent from an army surplus store. I pictured its previous life as perhaps part of the Officers' Mess, but a soldier friend put me right: it had been a latrine tent. Having been assured as I left the shop that it would be a simple matter for two people to put it up, we tried it out immediately on the lawn when I got home, and suffice it to say that the ensuing two hours were tough. But we managed it and stayed married. It was, from then on, up in the garden as a kitchen extension for most of the next five or six summers, and lit with candles at night it was particularly lovely.

Once we got over the horror of putting it up and taking it down, we plucked up our courage and stowed the tent, and the two girls, and a mountain of kit and provisions, in the car and drove uncomfortably to Suffolk. We put it up by arrangement in a remote stubble field above the River Deben, slung Mum's chandelier from the roof, put up camp beds and a trestle table and cooked a delicious supper. The friends whose field we were in came and ate with us as the sun went down and it was magic. And just as well we had used camp beds: it poured with rain in the night, but we were able to lie in our beds, pretty much dry, while a stream rushed beneath us.

✳

One of the best things about holidays abroad is the shopping – for food, of course, and all sorts of other things. Matthew is especially drawn to hardware stores, which makes for awkward but invaluable additions to one's luggage. A French *quincaillerie* will supply endless exciting seeds, which are easy to pack and make a vast difference to one's kitchen gardening, as they are often for better-tasting types of veg and fruit than we can buy at home. But his favourite purchase from one such shop was a grill with a handle, bought in Carentan around the time that camping seized his imagination. It is veteran of many picnics and campfires. I also love taking my cast-iron frying pan from Dehillerin in Paris, because it is so much nicer to use than any other in the world, but it weighs a ton so I need to be sure of a short walk or strong bearers.

Breakfast picnics in Norfolk in the past few years have taken a slightly regrettable turn, aesthetically speaking, since we discovered how easy it is to cook a vast post-swim breakfast on one or more chuck-away barbecues. They are horrid little things, but easy to balance on stones or whatever and thus avoid enraging farmers or National Trust wardens, who understandably take a dim view of campfires.

Pop's grandmother had a house above Treyarnon Beach, west of Padstow, where he spent his holidays as a boy. Here she taught him to surf and set fearless precedents for swimming in scary places.

Just along the cliffs from Treyarnon, to the west, there is one particular small, deep inlet, marked Fox Cove on the map. The path down to the sea is steep, shaley and slippery. When I peer over the rim of the cliff and look down, I find it hard to believe that we often used to scramble down there to swim, with our bathers, towels and jerseys for afterwards tied around our waists and shoulders. Sophy was given to panicky reversals in much easier situations than this – for example she threw a prolonged fit of screaming and running in circles, wind-milling her arms, when she thought that a grasshopper had landed in her hair. It hadn't. Yet Pop managed to carry her down to the beach in a sort of backwards piggyback, mostly on all fours. It was made a little easier by the fact that Fox Cove swims were saved for days when the weather somewhere far out to sea had changed, and the Atlantic became almost flat calm and so there was no surfing to be had. As a result, while we climbed down there were no waves crashing on the rocks, just a gently heaving, slapping swell, as if a vast whale was breathing close by. At low tide a small sandy beach was revealed with a huge grey rock parked down the middle of it, which looked like a submarine. As the tide rose high enough, Tom and I dived off it, then clambered back aboard and lay on its warm decks, making each other shiver with stories of the monster conger eels said to lurk in the deep rock pools.

An alternative outing was to walk around the coast in the other direction, to Booby's Bay, on the way to

Trevose Head. There at low tide the shallow, rocky pools and sandy ridges were scattered with entrancing shells, the most prized of which were tiny cowries which, despite being as fragile as – more fragile than – wrens' eggs, had survived their rough passage in the Gulf Stream for thousands of miles. We hunted in solitary competitive isolation, searching amongst the bladder-wrack, yellow winkles and smooth grey stones which, on this beach only, were striped with peppermint slips of white quartz; each of us keen to achieve the biggest haul before the sea crept back up the beach forcing a retreat, and then the walk home across the grassy thrift-scattered cliff tops. These pocketfuls of treasure harboured disgusting stinks unless you rinsed them a lot, then dried them out thoroughly on newspaper. It was then essential to make a shell box, so we laboured with UHU glue, sticking the shells crustily and thickly on cigar boxes, then slicking the result with clear varnish to make it look as if a wave had just washed over them.

Our stepmother Lucy did not have her first baby immediately. In fact we had her to ourselves for three years, which was lovely as she did lots of nice projects with us in those early days, particularly on holidays in Cornwall. I think that the shell boxes were inspired by her.

Tom and I were both very enthusiastic surfers, trying to emulate Pop who was – still is – very dashing in his wetsuit, far out beyond the break with all the tough young local guys on Malibu boards. We were **not** on big boards: we used old-fashioned, thin, curved wooden boards. I still do, if I can find one. They are rare now, abandoned for polystyrene, but back then, the waves were full of plucky types – the ladies wearing flowery rubber hats and bathing suits with modest skirt arrangements, and hardly a wetsuit in sight – and all of us on wooden boards.

The trick with surfing is first to get out to where the waves are breaking; then to hold your board up in front of you, base tucked into your tummy, jump forward in front of the next breaker, and paddle like fury so that you are moving fast enough for the wave to pick you up and whoosh you all the way to the frilly wavelets in the shallow water. In the heat of the moment, as the ridge of water looms towards you, terrifyingly powerful, it is all too easy to be holding your board upside-down, with the subtle curve of it pointing downwards. If you did make this mistake, the inverted board would plunge you underwater in a slow-motion scary somersault, probably digging into your tummy, causing agonising bruises. As well as the pain, we hated this especially because it made us look like complete beginners. Lucy had already told us about Californian surfers and chopped off our jeans to imitate their look, and now she came up with a cool solution to the upside-down-and-spluttering-and-writhing-in-agony problem. She painted big fat arrows and the word 'Up' on the front of our boards so we couldn't mistake which side to jump onto. Thinking about that now, maybe she thought we were really stupid and inclined to use the board backwards as well as upside-down. Never mind, the boards looked great.

During all of these holidays a redoubtable lady called Phyllis ruled the kitchen at Treyarnon. She kept control through the hatch. Each meal was a pantomime of controlled rage in the dining room, where my great-grandmother (when Pop was young), then Kelburn Granny, and latterly Lucy, our stepmother, simply yearned for a cup of coffee still hot; while in the kitchen Phyllis muttered warlike threats and did battle with the coughing water supply, the electric plugs which spat blue sparks, and what she saw as our excessive demands on her supplies. While tempers simmered, Tom and I would entertain each other by seeing how rude a burping noise we could make pouring glasses of water from the Plymouth Gin jugs, also known as glug-glug jugs. These fish-shaped jugs, dreamed up – for the pub trade, presumably – by some early incarnation of my designer friend Terry, trap liquid in the curved tail of the fish to make dramatic gurgles when tilted.

Phyllis was a fiery red-headed Cornish girl who had married the woodman at Glynn, the Vivian estate outside Bodmin where Kelburn Granny grew up. She looked after us children frequently and told us family stories. She had a kind heart – very – and a soft spot for a good-looking boy, which was lucky for Tom. She also had the silkiest skin, freckled like the cowries we hunted in Booby's Bay, and she hugged you kindly if you woke all confused and saddened to heartbreak by the awful mewling of the herring gulls on the next door roof, on a rainy afternoon.

Phyllis let me help her when she was making Cornish pasties for our lunch and I thought she probably really was Mrs Tiggywinkle, because she lived in an impossibly romantic little wooden house, all overgrown with honey-suckle and roses, in the woods at Cardinham, where she had to get all her water in a bucket from the well in the garden. We loved going there and I don't remember being at all frightened by the slow-worms on the paths there. They were tame compared to congers, I guess.

CORNISH PASTIES

* * *

Makes 4 large pasties

For the pastry, put a 100g block each of hard margarine and lard into the freezer and leave until frozen solid. Sift 450g strong white flour and a big pinch of salt into a large bowl and grate in the frozen margarine and lard. Mix in with your fingers, then stir in 175ml cold water with a round-bladed knife to make a dough. Knead briefly on a floured surface until smooth, wrap in clingfilm and chill for 1 hour. For the filling, cut 450g trimmed beef skirt into 5mm pieces. Dice 225g peeled swede and 750g peeled potatoes into the same-sized pieces and mix together with 225g chopped onion, some salt and plenty of black pepper. Cut the pastry into four and roll each piece out into a 20cm circle. Pile the filling to one side of each circle, brush the edge of the pastry with water and bring the other half over the filling so that the edges meet.

Press together well and then crimp. Place on a buttered baking sheet and chill for 1 hour. Brush with beaten egg, make three small slits in the top of each one and bake at 180°C/160°C fan/gas 4 for 1 hour until richly golden.

These ones are man-sized. Phyllis used to make them smaller, cutting the pastry circles by running a knife around a tea saucer (about 10cm diameter), which would make 7–8 pasties using the same ingredients.

AN OFFICE IN CHELSEA

So, that's the thing. Do you have that?

I am having dinner in a restaurant in Chelsea with a fellow lodger in my cousin's house just off the Kings Road. Jean-Marie and I usually pass on the stairs, or make each other coffee sometimes, but he must have noticed that I was wolfishly hungry and the fridge empty, and he kindly asked me to go with him to have supper with his boss. The fish we have just eaten for a main course was delicious, we have had a funny, friendly time and Jean-Marie has mostly listened while Franco quizzed me about the pottery. Now I'm feeling a bit spaced-out as the result of a day delivering orders over a wide area from Bristol to Canterbury in a Luton truck. And I

51

have just noticed that Jean-Marie has incredibly smiley crinkly brown eyes, now looking expectantly at me.

I make an effort and pull back into the conversation, and my mind bounces around the half-heard question. I really think: no, I don't have that. Franco's question is quite insistent,

I mean it. If you carry on, if you take your business seriously, if it keeps on growing, then you will one day have to make a hard decision, or several of them. People will be angry with you. Maybe they will really hate you.

God. I hope not. I can't possibly imagine that. My whole life is about doing the thing to make people like me, so that won't happen.

Well, yes. I guess I might make that decision.

I lie and smile. Trying to please Franco and say what he wants to hear. But he is not to be deflected.

I mean it. It always gets ugly at some point. Money changes all your relationships. You will be so surprised to find out who really approves of success. And who is working, as opposed to who is just mucking about.

He is getting abstract.

The business is now just me, as Alex and I have parted and we have managed to reach an agreement. True, that was a bit tense to negotiate, but we did it, and now he is a full-time photographer, and what was Brixton Spongeware is formally Emma Bridgewater, sole trader. And sole trader is what I feel like, as most days I work

16 hours. I can't stretch to picturing a situation involving other people who, in Franco's better understanding, will very soon be putting in similar hours. It just feels like a wild, wobbly balancing act I'm performing, very much on my own, with the main worry being – can I keep going? Will I manage to collect enough from my outstanding accounts to pay the factory bill at the end of the month? So why worry about an unimaginable future dilemma?

I yawn and mutter something incoherent. Franco starts to say something, then stops and smiles instead and says,

Hey, you guys are exhausted. Go home now, I'll see you tomorrow JM. No, I will get this, my treat. You are doing really well – good luck.

Without mentioning it, JM holds my arm as we walk home. We talk about Franco and his generosity and kindness, then back in Wellington Square we kiss goodnight. I thank him for saving me from starvation. I am curiously aware still of the prints of his fingers on my arm.

He disappears upstairs, and I have to pile boxes into towers to reach the sofa bed at the back of the double room on the ground floor, which is my office, warehouse and bedroom. Tonight Desmond is sleeping in the single bed in the front half of the room as he has some American cousins in all the upstairs beds. I'm too tired to think about how this is going to work in the morning. I'm almost certain that I have a New York store coming in to look at the sample collection at nine, and it's behind the bed Des will be sleeping in, and he is still out now. Too bad. I simply must go to sleep, and I dive into unconsciousness on the sofa among the boxes.

I wake up and sit bolt upright – Barneys are definitely coming at nine. What's the time? It's only quarter past eight. With relief I calculate swiftly that I have time to dress and tidy all the junk out of the front room before they arrive. But first I had better make some tea for Des to get him moving. The milk is off. I dash back down to my room, scramble into some passable clothes, hunt for cash, rush to the baker's at the bottom of the square, then back to take Des his first cup of tea.

Des. DESMOND! You have to wake up. I'm so sorry, but you have to.

Mmmm, wa? Ah, tea, good.

And he turns over and goes back to sleep. I pile the box towers even higher in the back room, still leaving a tempting passageway, hoping I might manage to entice Desmond to the sofa and almost out of harm's way. The front room is still a bit rough-looking, so I dash down to the basement and pick some camellia branches in the back garden, apologising to Chloe, Desmond's mother, in my head, as I know she would rather I asked first. The green shiny leaves in a pretty jug make the room look even grubbier and I wish there were time or Hoover bags so I could have a go at the carpet. I open the window.

Des, please *will you get out of bed? I've made you some more tea.*

Snuffling noises and small signs of life. Entirely undisturbed by my thundering about and proffered pleas and threats, my landlord sleeps on. There is no chance of getting him up in time – they are due in a minute and bound to be prompt. Instead I make do with emptying ashtrays, and putting pencils and sponge-cutting kit onto the table, and picking up most of the scraps of cut sponge which litter the floor. Leaning over him, I tidy the samples and remove a rank-looking cottage cheese pot, a Mars bar wrapper and a Marlboro packet from amongst the new designs. Desmond looks like Tommy Brock, apparently asleep but not reliably so. Can I trust him to stay there now? The bed looks rumpled, the blankets a bit holey. I cast about for something to throw over him, but it is too late; the doorbell rings. I can hear American voices on the doorstep. I push his clothes under the bed as a final touch.

I think it was definitely a first for the buyers. I apologised for Desmond's sleeping form, then sat them down and tried to talk them through the collection. The two ladies got over their amazement and stopped goggling. Then, in the kindly way of Americans, they became concerned – was my cousin well?

Surely he must not be. What could we do for him?

I assured them briskly that Desmond was fine, just tired. He must need coffee, they insisted. With a sigh I stopped trying to tempt them with spongeware as Desmond, perked up by the word coffee, started to stir.

Ah yes, coffee. Mmm, yes.

OK. Desmond, stay there. Shall I make us all coffee?

Definitely.

I had no confidence that the situation was in hand. I had just better be quick and leave them with him for as short a time as possible.

I was back with a tray in less than no time, but not soon enough. Desmond was wide awake and discussing my price list with the nice ladies, and suggesting that if they ordered several hundred dollars' worth, they would be able to ask me for a decent discount. He agreed, or maybe even suggested, that the prices were pretty high. And said that he reckoned that they should be able to persuade me to do a special design. Before I had poured the coffee he was on first name terms and talking Manhattan neighbourhoods.

I hastily filled in an order form for the buyers, noted the existing designs that they might like and hoped to bring the meeting to an end. But in vain. They stayed an hour, made extensive plans (prompted by my cousin) for the sample designs – plural – that I would do for them to see five days from now, just before they flew back home. Eventually I hustled them out, said goodbye on the steps and apologised for my unorthodox office arrangements.

Oh no, they chorused. *Dermot is just darling.*

When they were safely on their way, I went back to find Desmond rootling through my wardrobe. He waved a monkey boot at me and said he'd borrow them. Then went upstairs to have a bath.

I lay on the sofa for a few minutes feeling faint with annoyance, and also maybe hunger. I wondered how I'd get the Barneys designs done in time, and whether Jean-Marie had done any breakfast shopping.

Later on, around seven that evening, while I was still hunched over the soldering iron, cutting new sponges to send to Sam's decorators, Desmond limped in.

It's jolly annoying of you not to tell me that those boots are too small for me. My feet are really painful. Shall we have a drink now?

WE LIVED ON
LOVE STREET

M UM HAD A GENIUS for picnics. She loved food
in all circumstances – was very greedy, extremely
generous and boundlessly hospitable – and many of the
best feasts she served up we ate out of doors. She understood completely that life should be full of fun. She was
the author of so many slightly unlikely meals in novel
places, such as a Scottish beach where the whole Sunday
lunch in roasting tins and china bowls was carried down
a cliff path and eaten, still a bit warm, after a refreshingly
scary swim; or breakfast cooked on a bucket barbecue
ferried out on a sailing boat to the island at Brancaster;
or crab sandwiches whilst sheltering from the east wind
amongst the crab boats on the stones of Cley beach. We

ate fish and chips in the car at Minster Lovell in the rain; bread and cheese and hard-boiled eggs on Royston Heath; and thermos tea and lardy cake in some bluebell woods by Islip, outside Oxford.

This annual ritual of tea in a bluebell wood touched some deep well of pleasure for her, and it still seems important to me to know where the best bluebells are and, if at all possible, to make the pilgrimage and experience the cathedral-like awe you can't help but feel as you lie listening to the cuckoo in the echoing groves. Mum or her friend Felicity had found this particular wood with its mesmerising drifts of misty blue glimpsed through the trees. We returned one day after school and, leaving the cars parked rakishly on the verge, climbed through the fence and walked in search of a spot for picnicking. Trespassing was a notion Mum usually ignored in a rather vague way, which made me a bit jumpy on these types of outing, but it was she who beat a retreat this time when Tom and his friend Charlie found a laddish camp with beer bottles and porn mags under a birdcherry tree, and brought some back to the picnic where she and Felicity were feeding their babies. She was not fussed, but her distaste was evident – the strong spells of happy magic she wove around us were maybe more fragile to her than I realised. The ugliness of the world she set aside: Mum was expert at ignoring things and people who bored or offended her; she wafted above unpleasantness, insisting that most of the world was lovely and fun, and things would go well. Living under this spell was especially cosy and warm and enchanted. But if forced to have contact with nastiness, she slid down from the clouds with a bump, in this case bundling the picnic into the baskets, and all of us back into the cars, very decisively.

The picnics of my childhood which I ate without Mum were never as good as those served up by her with a flourish from the red canvas sailing bag, or from her selection of baskets. This may also have been partly because she kept no Tupperware or biscuit tins, and tinfoil was a bit of an extravagance, so my lunch for the school trip to the Greenwich Observatory and the *Cutty Sark* was a far cry from the packed lunches of my friends. I remember delicious but very crumbly lettuce and Marmite sandwiches (the bread being home-made), baggily wrapped in a supermarket plastic carrier, with dried apricots as pudding and an enamel cup to fill from a tap. Had such a thing been proffered then, she would have disapproved wildly of water in plastic bottles. She was pretty anti lemon barley water and Ribena (sooo expensive), let alone fizzy drinks (we only ever had Coke at parties) – perish the thought. In this, as in several other food prejudices, her hippy tendencies led her to convictions 40 years ago that have since become mainstream. She made her own bread (fairly regularly and always brown, like the spelt loaf) and yoghurt, and muesli (sometimes), and believed that refined white sugar and flour were likely to provoke mood swings and difficult behaviour. We ate a lot of lentils, beans, chickpeas and cracked wheat, all of which featured in picnics as salads and hummus just as often as she served them up hot at home.

Across the Downs, riding along the crests of the bosomy hills of Berkshire, Oxfordshire and Wiltshire, runs a mysterious and lovely track called the Ridgeway. This ancient road was often on Mum's mind. She encouraged Nell and Clover to do day-long rides, dropping them off at the Uffington White Horse with a picnic in a rucksack, their destination Barbary Castle, where she would meet them with the trailer at dusk. After Mum's accident we celebrated Clover's sixteenth birthday on a chilly April night on the Ridgeway, camping at Wayland's Smithy as the ghosts of Roman legionaries tramped past on the track. We cooked sausages on a fire and drank tequila to keep warm, which may well account for the ghosts.

*

The best of the picnics – the picnic to define all picnics – was on a June weekend during the heatwave of 1976, in the water meadows by the Cherwell, and was a double birthday celebration. A big chattering party of about 20 people, plus dogs, and children buzzing around on bikes, walked through north Oxford and down Marston Ferry Road which, in the days before the by-pass, turned from road to lane as it passed the Cherwell School, then meandered between frothing hedges down past allotments, then through hay meadows to a ferry which bore passengers across the river to the garden of the Victoria Arms pub at Marston. Two large cold roast chickens, salad, mayonnaise, potatoes, strawberries, cream, bottles of wine and lemonade and a big squishy chocolate cake were all carried in a wheelbarrow, along with plates, glasses and cutlery. We spread rugs on the grass, ate, drank, and took a jug across on the ferry and bought beer at the pub when the wine ran out. Then in the shimmering heat of the afternoon everybody swam in the river, splashing and diving, or floating beneath the willow trees, dreaming, talking.

Because of the cattle in the meadows, we swatted at horseflies from time to time, but the afternoon was so dreamy that I remember that for once I scarcely minded them. I was even unmoved by Mum's terrible bathers. Her clothes were eccentric, and generally wonderful. She often wore long skirts, embroidered shirts, long flowery dresses as well as jeans or denim skirts, clogs, espadrilles, big hats – the look was picturesque. And if she presented a very different picture to that of the other mums at the High School, I knew that she looked just right in the gardens of New College or bicycling down St Giles. And she was certainly perfectly dressed for a hay meadow. But when it came, as it often did, to swimming, I usually fell into standard teenage squirming embarrassment as she wound an African cloth around herself and launched into the water, though that day everything seemed right. And as it was so hot everyone swam, and mostly in their pants or naked; it was too hot not to, and much too hot and lovely to care.

Our house in Oxford was full of lodgers; by the time Mum and Rick moved to Wiltshire, we had colonised two thirds of the house, but when we moved in, the top floor was let as a flat and four big rooms on the first floor were rented to undergraduates. This was a source of endless pleasure for Tom and me, to whom they were almost always kind and patient, despite the fact that we must have been pesky nuisances, unaware of the stress of exams and very interested in them and all their goings on. There was an exotic lady called Erica whose parrot imitated laughter, often recognisable as mimicry, and until the fleas drove Mum to banish the bird, we spent hours trying to make the parrot giggle. One summer when we came back from our holidays, we found that a friend of a lodger had started a motorbike repair business on the landing; and another had taken advantage while the coast was clear and painted her entire room, including fireplace and ceiling, a very deep purple. We begged Mum to keep the colour after the lodger eventually left.

Some of the undergraduates who rented rooms became lifelong friends; others came and went almost unremarked. Some were honest – one sweet girl told Mum that the gas meter was faulty; another, in a wheelchair, stopped paying her rent and eventually told Mum she must put her out on the pavement and call a social worker to come and re-house her.

The porch was overhung with a big choisya and stacked with bikes, a pram, a pushchair and roller skates. Loads of people had keys, and they and their friends came and went and played music and borrowed the telephone. They did this last infrequently, as the telephone was in the kitchen and deliberately difficult to use for long calls. The front door was usually locked, at night at least, so when I forgot my key and came home after Mum had gone to bed, which happened easily as she was always keener on early morning than late night, I would have to climb in through a window around the back and negotiate the huge wooden throne that covered the downstairs loo. Security was not tight.

After his Finals, Rick trained as a TV director and went to work for Granada. In due course we moved into the upstairs bedrooms ourselves and the undergraduates retreated to the attic at the top of the house. Lodgers, who had been full-time, departed, and in their place came PGs (short for 'paying guests') during the week and in the term time only, mostly sixth-formers at the High School who slept in Tom's room while he was away at school, and shared with me. The landing and stairs were re-carpeted; a loo with a sink outside it gave way to a bathroom; rooms were painted; gas meters banished; and Mum bought a collection of Victorian brass beds to replace the terrible lumpy old single beds donated by great-aunts and foraged in house clearances. Now at weekends my room, which had two large beds, was always full of girls staying before and after parties, and hoping that Alan Bates or Albert Finney or Diana Quick would come to lunch on Sunday (which happened from time to time). The sofas in the playroom were often draped with bodies of unconscious boyfriends in the mornings, yet Mum and Rick almost never, in my memory, got cross about any of this.

The house in Rawlinson Road was a domain of love and laughter, picnics and parties, and Mum was Prospero in a Turkoman robe with a sparkly belt and red suede boots, and Rick's records, such as The Doors, were the soundtrack: Love Street sounded just like Rawlinson Road to me.

✳

Thirty years or so later, when Matthew and I lived in a shabby but friendly old rectory in Norfolk, our teenage daughters brought numerous friends to stay, sometimes for weeks on end. We loved it, missed them when they went away, always encouraged them and cheerfully cooked everlasting breakfasts. Because teenagers have magical power. When they arrive in your house, it's as if a flock of angels has landed fluttering and chattering on your sofas. They are beautiful and wonderful. Is it because they are poised between the careless, busy raptures of childhood and the focus and action of adult life? I don't know, but they are in a state of change, full of potential and unsure how to use their power. It seems to me that teenagers are at an important juncture, and this cross-roads is a wonderful place to stop, set up camp, and talk a lot, about everything.

COLD ROAST CHICKEN AND GREEN MAYONNAISE

* * *

Turn a chicken (as free-range and corn-fed as possible) onto its breast and cut either side of the backbone with scissors or poultry shears. Open up, flip back over and press down firmly on the breast-bone to flatten the bird. Rub the chicken all over with a little soft butter and season well. Put 1–2 thick slices of lemon, 2 bruised unpeeled cloves of garlic, 2 anchovy fillets and a small bunch of tarragon (or thyme) into the centre of an oiled roasting tin, then put the chicken on top, and drizzle over a little olive oil and a splash of white wine. Roast at 200°C/180°C fan/gas 6 for 45–50 minutes until cooked through and the skin is brown. For the mayonnaise, put 2 egg yolks, 2 teaspoons of white wine vinegar and ½ teaspoon of salt into a bowl and mix together. Very slowly whisk in 300ml sunflower oil or olive oil (you can use an electric hand whisk if you like) until you have a thick mayonnaise. Stir in some finely chopped herbs. I like parsley, chervil and coriander.

THOUSANDS OF MILES AND
TOO MUCH COUNTRY MUSIC

IN THE FIRST YEAR of the business, I drove a Mini Metro, a present from my father. It was not glamorous or cool, but it was reliable and surprisingly capacious. I could fit 12 trays of rattling ware into it if I folded the seats, and that was very useful at the beginning when ferrying down to Brixton the first batches of ware (fired for me by Sam) for experiments in decoration.

But when it came to delivering the first orders, and from then on, I was looking at transporting 50 or more trays at a time, and I needed something bigger. Once again I turned to Alex for advice – having an older, practical boyfriend was invaluable – and he sent me off to a van hire business under some arches somewhere in south

London to hire a cheap Transit. This seems to loom large in my memory so I guess it was simply frightening; I was very stretched financially, the blokes who rented me a van every few weeks (for it quickly became a regular part of life) were rough, the vans were cheap and unreliable and I frequently broke down. I joined the AA and made liberal use of their services. Changing tyres almost lost its horror for me. My map reading went from tragic to efficient.

I even got good at mending cassette tapes when they twisted or snapped – using a corner of a ring-pull as a screwdriver, you can open the cassette and wind the tape back onto its sprocket. You use a packing knife to slice out the stretched tape which jams in the player and causes havoc, then splice the tape back together with Sellotape, trim the sides clean with the knife, screw the cassette back together and it plays like new – with just a little hiccup in Linda Ronstadt's voice to show where the operation took place. I only mention this to explain just how important country music was to me. I listened to Radio Two, Radio Three, local radio when desperate and thousands of hours of Radio Four, but if you spend a lot of time in the car, the repeats really start to get to you. And it always seems to be *Money Box*, or *Does He Take Sugar?* or *You and Yours* when you need distraction or amusement rather than infuriation.

✳

Ken loved making mix tapes almost more than he loved Mum's bread toasted on a Sunday morning; his taste is wide, his record collection enormous, but his predilection for country music is simply inexhaustible. Thanks to him, I think positively of pretty much any song that tells a story. He seems to have bunched a huge range of genre music under the spangly awning of 'country', which makes sense to me – just as long as it made getting back into the van with a paper cup of coffee late at night something I could almost look forward to. So his tapes would feature all of these singers and bands: Willie Nelson, Gram Parsons, Tim Hardin, Emmylou Harris, Townes Van Zandt, Bob Dylan, Rodney Crowell, Johnny Cash, Kris Kristofferson, Dolly Parton, John Prine, Bruce Springsteen, Van Morrison, Elvis Costello, Janis Joplin, The Band, Steve Earle, the Fureys, and then some more Emmylou. And also Elvis Presley. Ken has a better ear for a segue than anyone, and he sometimes reached peaks of creative selecting and juxtaposing, the best ever being a tape inspired by the American South, with love letters from the battlefields of the Civil War spoken over haunting music, as well as the Judds and Michelle Shocked.

Maybe it helps that so many country songs are about travelling, giving an easy synergy with driving, lending the faraway thrill of Route 66 to the M6, and bringing something of the roadside diner on a lonely prairie highway to South Mimms service station. But it seems to be a more sustaining connection than that. I still have lots of the tapes that Ken made me, and sometimes I find a machine so I can play them and experience that nostalgic hiss, and the rush of remembering how excited and how driven I felt. The yearning feeling at the heart of country music exactly matches how I felt – still feel – about life, and family, and business. Cars stopped being fitted with cassette players, and Ken has not learned about downloading – neither have I – so I took to buying CDs and added Lucinda Williams, Lyle Lovett, Po' Girl, Corb Lund, Alison Krauss, Gillian Welch, Kelly Willis and still more Emmylou to the litter of broken cases on the floor of one car after another.

In 2001, when Michael was just 3 months old, I realised that I had to get back into the company and take an active role again after 10 years or so during which family life had taken priority. We had just bought a remote and run-down old rectory in north Norfolk, and it was heavenly. But as it was to transpire, I was always driving away from it, leaving the sweet peas and the roses, the cherry trees and the chicken runs behind, and flooring it towards the West Midlands. I could never have done this without The Be Good Tanyas, The McGarrigle Sisters and Emmylou. Yearly I drove something more than 50,000 miles commuting between Wickmere, Hanley and Fulham, and I still dream about stretches of the road through the Fens or the Leicestershire Wolds – always with a soundtrack of harmonising voices singing of love and loss and longing; of wayward men, bad choices and second chances.

*

Thanks to Ken, country music seems to be a family soundtrack. My youngest sister Clover went to Oxford, then, at a loose end after Finals, she went to America with a few hundred pounds that she had saved up, and a handful of contacts. She didn't love New York, so she set out on a bus to find excitement in Texas. Where she hoped that she might be able to get a job as a cowgirl; and about three months later she wrote that she really was wearing chaps and a Stetson and swinging a lasso.

On a sudden impulse I booked a flight to Dallas. Matt was happy to hold the fort and I was not going to miss seeing Clover's Wild West career for myself. Well, I almost did. There was a pile-up on the motorway and I didn't make my flight. I threw myself on the mercy of the British Airways desk and they kindly gave me a ticket for a flight just leaving for. . . Atlanta. As I hurried towards check-in, I dived into a bookshop and bought a *Rough Guide to the USA*. On the flight it dawned on me quite how far I would have to drive to get to Amarillo, which was Clover's nearest big town. It was over a thousand miles, and my return flight from Dallas was just a week away. Oh blimey.

But it turned out to be a wonderful, completely exhilarating drive across half of America on my own – surfing the radio stations; driving through the landscape of so many of my very best book, film and music experiences; eating in diners; eavesdropping on farmers, truck drivers and other travellers; and sleeping in sleazy roadside motels. Clover had given me good directions for finding the ranch and told me that the last 20 miles or so were 'off the pavement', which sounded suitably odd. I turned off the tarmac onto a dirt road feeling undeterred; I figured that I could think of friends in, say, Scotland who lived a long way from the main road. But this was somehow so much wilder, emptier. There were nothing but miles of red dirt and mesquite bushes, and once I had to stop as a number of rangy-looking black cattle milled across the track in front of me. My hire car bounced and slewed through the deep dust and dry washes and I lost track of forks and turnings. I was lost. I felt concerned, then relieved when I unexpectedly saw a caravan with some dogs dozing around its door. Relief turned to slightly giggly terror as I approached and all the dogs sprang up growling. Was I walking into a horror movie? Would I be chopped up with a chainsaw, never heard of again? But the man who stepped out was polite, if a bit sleepy, and he put me back on the track to the ranch. No shotgun, no rattlesnakes pinned on the fence, all fine.

I ploughed on, the road rose, then went over a crest and down into a canyon. I could see the ranch in the distance. As I pulled into the gateway there were two boys, obviously cowboys in their hats, boots and jeans, sitting on the wall above, chewing straws. I looked again, and the boys leapt down and ran towards the car – it was Clover and Nell. I had not known Nell would be there too; it was perfect. We fell on each other and kissed and hugged, then I stood back to look at the extraordinarily wonderful place that Clover had found. She had gone from day to day when she first got to Texas, doing casual work on one dude ranch and another, then she was galvanised into finding a job on a big prestigious ranch by the derisory attitude of a cowboy whilst two-stepping one night. He said he dared say she might get a job rounding up sheep on a lesbian ranch in East Texas, but she was never going to work on the King Ranch. She had mentioned this legendary spread, down near San Antonio, because she had almost secured an introduction to the foreman on the King. The cowboy's careless chauvinism fired her determination; she was definitely going to get that job!

As it turned out, she was reading *Horseman, Pass By* on the bus down south when she realised that even more than the King Ranch, she needed to see the great JA

Ranch, star of many of Larry McMurtry's novels. So she turned around, went up to the Panhandle, tracked down the foreman of the JA Ranch in Clarendon and persuaded him to give her a try-out. He said that it was up to the owner. The owner said that she could try out if Billy, the foreman, said she was up to it, if she really wanted such a hard job. And she pulled it off. She was to spend nearly a year there before she left, having won her spurs, broken broncs, killed rattlesnakes with a broom, learned to rope and haze, and having made friends amongst the cowboys and their wives and girlfriends. She even made it into the ranch rodeo team before she left on a sudden unbearable wave of homesickness for the green, damp, gentle beauty of England.

Her bold adventure inspired me, as did Texas itself and the glimpse I had into life on the ranch, with its old-world courtesy and huge masculine pride. I felt privileged to be amongst men who worked the ranch in the old-fashioned way, handling themselves, their horses, their kit and the cattle with such strength and skill. Clover had proved herself in a man's world and, as I saw it, she lived the point that prejudice has to be a useful incentive, rather than a brake on your schemes.

So what was going on? Why all that driving? Well, I could see that with four children and a house badly in need of a new roof, we urgently needed to grow the company and make it more profitable. So I needed to get back into the swing of work, and I wanted to learn how to manage a company effectively myself, to buy back the shares parted with in the early years and energise the brand. It was not really an option to leave Norfolk, so instead I undertook to commute between the commercial office, in the basement below our shop on the Fulham Road, our factory in Stoke-on-Trent and home. My life became a hectic road movie with a nonstop country music soundtrack.

It was hard to wind up my courage to step forward but it was time to take control and shoulder my responsibility. For ten years Matt and I had been living in Norfolk, designing all the time, yes; creating and manning lots of trade fair stands, sometimes more than six in a year, in France and the US as well as in England; styling and designing the catalogues throughout – but neither of us actually ran the company in this time. In fact, since forming a partnership with Matthew and Marcus just before Elizabeth was born, I had been pretty preoccupied with family life. When Michael arrived something changed in me and I could feel a rising determination to make the company much larger, more profitable and more powerful. But for some time I wavered, totally unsure how to go about taking this momentous step.

The missing resolve came from an unexpected quarter. On a wintry February day I went to Billa Harrod's 'Snowdrop Morning'. Her house outside Holt seemed to stand in a snowdrift, as the galanthus of many varieties that she had planted over the years had naturalised and spread so enthusiastically. Billa was a heroine. She lived life with elegant, original and unshakeable independence. She set up and rocket-fuelled the Norfolk Churches Trust, a model of informed and loving conservation. Like most people, I was in awe of her and not a little scared; she could be very fierce if annoyed. In a chilly straggle her devotees wandered around the garden, crossing and re-crossing the little stream over rickety bridges and worshipping briefly at the pools of aconites beneath the trees. Indoors we made wet footprints on our way to the turquoise dining room for cups of tea and slices of cake. In the hall before we left she drew the raffle, standing by a round table in the middle of which was a huge, purple lustre punch bowl stuffed full with snowdrops. Before I left, I asked her how they all sat so prettily – why didn't the middle ones drown? She showed me that they stood on sodden, bunched-up newspaper. It was a piece of perfection. I thought about her determination to make good things happen in life, and the fog I'd been in cleared. If I wanted to make the company work, if I wanted to make good things happen, it was time to set aside my placatory habits. I would have to be uncompromising, like Billa. That was all.

Over the course of three or four years, painfully and not always with grace, I started to make headway. I was given lots of heroic support, and I weathered some epic rows; I made friends, asked favours, took on a bold, effective commercial director – my other Matthew – and, with his help, found a financial controller, a wonderful and redoubtable lady called Caryl who created strong accounts. We eventually gained some kind of real insight into what was happening in the factory, where there was a mixture of fantastic loyalty and predictable dishonesty going on. To assert better control throughout the company we moved half the staff from the factory office down to Fulham and learned the painful inside of the term 'restructuring'. The sales tripled, the factory remained hard to govern and there were difficult part-ings and hellish, frighteningly expensive, hours in lawyers' offices.

Alongside all the turmoil of running and growing the company, and building and managing a commercial team, we were also struggling to improve productivity and stock control in the factory. Meanwhile Matthew made a most wonderful studio in an outlying part of the factory and set about the vital central mission for the company, namely more and still more beautiful designs, now with a commercial brief.

*

At a certain point, perhaps in 2005 or 2006, the Potters' Union requested an interview. The content of our meeting was unimportant – we were paying over their recommendations and had no safety issues, so they had no specific requests for change – but the tone, the atmosphere, of the meeting shocked and haunted me. It made me realise what I had blithely ignored up to that point: that to some people, my project – my business – was offensive. No matter that I employed 70 people at the time. Their attitude was not, as I assumed it must be, 'Golly, that's great, how can we help you make that 140 jobs?' Instead they simply hated me for being a boss, and sought to gain what controls they might within the company.

And when the awful meeting was over I could see why I made them feel hot and furious. I hated my privileged situation at that moment, and felt apologetic and confused. But my embarrassment passed, and when it had, I still wanted to make jobs and try to save a small part of this beleaguered industry.

It seems that there is still a need – and also exciting scope – to develop a dynamic relationship between the unions who bring their proud history, traditions and skills – and entrepreneurs keen to make new products in this country.

At the time of my first encounter with the unions we were experiencing runaway success with a design of Pink Hearts, and I still relish the contrast between our girly patterns and their rugged halo of soot and clay dust. I guess it is not surprising that two such contrasting groups should find each other completely surprising.

I fell in and out of love frequently between my sixth-form years and my marriage ten years later. I could lose my heart for rock star legs, for a husky voice, for an American accent, for a blushing seriousness about theology as much as for a sweeping batting innings. In my second year at university I met Alex and moved in with him because he could strip down an engine, he knew when the big end of the car had gone, and he was generally brilliant with a spanner. When I'd realised, two years later, that this was not enough to ensure true love forever, I had a passionate, thrilling love affair with a Frenchman. Then there was Marcus. He was brooding and romantic, his sisters were both friends of mine and they jokingly encouraged my helpless love for their little brother. As well as being the incarnation of His Grace, the Duke of Avon, straight out of the pages of *These Old Shades* (at least it seemed so to me, obsessed as I was with Georgette Heyer, loving her books for their saturnine, aloof heroes), he was also funny and sweet, but always elusive, and I think, fundamentally relieved when I stopped chasing him around the pubs of Notting Hill and introduced him to Matthew.

But before Matt came on the scene, about six months after I wrote my first invoice, the bank manager lost patience with me and demanded to know what was going on. I had effectively been trading out of my own current account, with no formal arrangement at the bank. I did not know how to write the business plan he wanted, but there was at least an order book and about 120 shops, active accounts who were now ordering and re-ordering from me. Marcus had experience of business so I begged him to help me. He wrote a plan which, whilst not showing any likelihood of making a big profit, at least created order out of the stressful optimism in my head. There were some plus points, such as the fact that Sam allowed me 30 days to pay his bills, whilst I had agreed terms of 28 days with my customers. Probably the most significant fact was that my stuff was very expensive, roughly twice the price of most comparable earthenware, which was a brake on what might otherwise have been a complete muddle.

We were nervous, waiting in the marble hall of the Royal Bank of Scotland. I really needed the bank to grant me a business overdraft and this was the first time

I had ever stopped to think that the business was not inevitable. There was a real possibility that the bank manager might say no. My stepfather had kindly sent me off to see his accountant a few weeks previously. The accountant was appalled by the liability I was creating and strenuously advised me to cease trading immediately. Perhaps the bank would say the same.

Mr Tolfrey's office was large and formal and designed to inspire awe as well as confidence. The crazy rumpus ride of the past six months, during which I had been borne on a tide of adrenalin and excitement, suddenly stopped; I felt as if I was in the headmistress' study and I braced myself for the row. We sat opposite Mr Tolfrey with about an acre of mahogany between us and he fired questions at us. Marcus kicked me whenever I ran on too long; he was calm and confident about the figures and had answers to most of the questions about margins, payment terms, debt levels and running costs. Suffice it to say, Marcus won Mr Tolfrey over and we got an official overdraft. This all took place in Burlington Gardens, in a building which is now the flagship branch of Abercrombie & Fitch. When I walked in recently, I was surprised to find gorgeous scantily-clad models writhing in near darkness in the very room in which Marcus and I had set out our plans for the business.

TO THE MEMORY
OF CHARLOTTE

THE STAFFORDSHIRE POTTERS do not have a monopoly on commemorative wares, but they have been very good at this genre and developed it to considerable commercial significance. In Stoke-on-Trent a royal wedding, jubilee or baby is more than a cue for a street party; these events make local jobs and prosperity.

From the outset of commercial production, there was obviously a big appetite for pottery mugs and jugs which exhorted emotional responses through lavish criticism, praise and dire warnings. In a way that we find unfamiliar, the taste seems to have been very attuned to mourning. One death in particular inspired widespread national grief, and lots of commemorative china: namely that of Princess

Charlotte, daughter of George IV, who died in childbirth in 1817. Much ware 'To the Memory of Charlotte' survives. Some friends gave my mother, whose name is Charlotte, a bowl, cup and saucer trio as a jokey present when she left Cambridge.

On a Monday morning in November 1991 Mum made us all breakfast, saw us off to London, or to school, or left us to revise at home, then with enormous pleasure went off alone for a day's hunting. When her horse slipped on the road later that morning, she fell on her head, suffered very serious head injuries, spent nearly three months in a coma, and woke up gradually to a dreadfully changed life, with no more jokes. She came back to Minety less than four months after that blithe morning, but she never came home. For two years we all tried to look after her, among her friends and neighbours and all her things. Nell and Clover, just 15 and 17 at the time, bore the lion's share of the caring. Then two years later Rick quietly and sensibly decided that whatever recovery poor Mum might make, the rest of her family would pay too high a price. So he sold the house, she went into the first of several nursing homes, and life moved on. With a jagged hole in the middle of it for all of us.

I think I was lucky; I had known her the longest, I was married, I had two children of my own and I had already started my business, so I had plenty to get on with. But the pain of losing her is still raw, and it often springs out to ambush me from something of hers – a song, a scarf or a plate can detonate a landmine, any day. From the very beginning my designs were inspired by her, and since that frightful day, really all of my work has been To the Memory of Charlotte.

Memorialising powerful politicians and criminal celebrities, in its pre-Victorian phase commemorative pottery went hand in hand with the cartoonists and broadsheet journalists of the day; the look and tone of political commentary was fierce, satirical, critical, fearless. This confident stance seems to lose its swagger in the course of the nineteenth century, settling into a huge commercial output of models of infamous murder scenes (like the Red Barn) or notorious villains (including Bellingham, who murdered the now-unremembered Prime Minister Spencer Perceval) or, best of all, murderesses (such as Charlotte Corday, who stabbed the revolutionary Marat in his bath), all of them well-known in their day and satisfying contemporary gory tastes.

And in the twentieth century commemorative wares grow yet tamer in tone, indicating a dwindling appetite for politics, murders and scandals. The Profumo Affair generated much written commentary, but I have yet to find a mug emblazoned 'He would, wouldn't he?', which is a pity. Both World Wars made for lots of pottery,

as did each royal wedding, funeral or coronation –
keep an eye out for the interesting and anachronistic
mugs made before his sudden abdication to mark the
coronation of Edward VIII; there were thousands made
in advance. You will see in antique shops and on mantelpieces plenty of mugs to remember explorers, and many
sportsmen (especially cricketers for some reason), but
you have to wait for Fluck and Law, in partnership with
Wade Pottery, in the 1980s to reconnect with fierce and
funny commemorative ware. The creators of *Spitting
Image* puppets combine acute physical observation with
great – and now rare – modelling skills, and I wish very
much that I owned a Neil Kinnock egg cup. The Fluck
and Law pottery goes a little way to offset the lame
quality of most of the recent commemorative wares – I
think we have simply to draw a veil over most of the
mass market commemorative mugs from about 1975
onwards, for Prince Charles, Prince Andrew, Princess
Diana and Queen Elizabeth the Queen Mother. They
are, for the most part, just too feeble.

It is of course true that the prestigious makers,
Wedgwood, Spode and Royal Crown Derby, shake themselves and rise to royal occasions to produce small,
expensive editions of something beautiful, but not much
inspiration for the wider market. However, the recent
spate of royal celebrations have come at a better time,
and I think that Stoke is once again waking up to the

huge commercial and artistic possibilities of commemorative ware. At Emma Bridgewater, for example, we sold large numbers of mugs marking the Queen's Diamond Jubilee in 2012. But we are, alas, completely unable to decide how to, or indeed whether to, remember Margaret Thatcher. I think that Josiah is a bit disgusted from beyond the grave.

Right next door to commemorative ware, which encourages us all to join in with great events from Nelson's victory at Aboukir Bay to Elizabeth II's Diamond Jubilee, I would place the wares which we commission to mark the landmark events in our own lives. When I look at my favourite jug, marked 'Archibald Thomson Macmerry', or just a little Victorian china mug which says 'Elizabeth', I love the connection to an unknown person, long dead. I love the names, the script, the decoration, the date, the event – or indeed the complete lack of it, leaving the name to stand alone – invoking that long-gone wedding or baptism. Better still, this tradition is alive and flourishing. Indeed, there is a timeless pleasure in commissioning something completely personal. We don't lose confidence in this arena, even if we are completely uncertain about how to remember the Iron Lady; we feel confident to greet the birth of a nephew, the wedding of a sister or any such event by having a plate or teapot made to mark the date.

One of my godmothers gave me a christening mug. It is bone china with flowers and my name and the date of my baptism in twirly gold writing. Also, Tom, Sophy and I each had a sturdy little striped earthenware mug bearing our name. Both items were great favourites in my childhood. Why? I think that it is as if my baptism or even my name is made slightly more real because so thoughtfully incorporated into a pretty thing that might well exist on a shelf somewhere long after I am gone. Next door to a mug for Churchill, or Gladstone, or Ellen Terry, or even Elvis. It's a tiny bid for immortality.

The royal family is sometimes referred to as the Ministry for Happiness. I did not know how apt this was until we had a royal visit to our factory. It was in March 2011, and the Prince of Wales and the Duchess of Cornwall were to visit Stoke-on-Trent to mark the centenary of the federation of the six towns into a city. Arnold Bennett was making a typically dry joke when he excluded Fenton and christened Stoke 'the Five Towns', and his sniping is indicative of the crotchety relationship that still persists between the towns, 100 years after all differences were to have been drowned out in civic harmony. As well as a session in the Lord

Mayor's Parlour, a gala lunch and much ribbon cutting, the royal visitors were to tour several potteries, and we were thrilled to be approached to see if we would like to be included. There was no hesitation from us; we said 'yes please' straight away.

Our entire female staff fell in love with the royal protection team as they arranged with us exactly what the factory tour would be like: where the party would stop, for how many minutes, who would be standing at each spot – all was pre-arranged. The team swept the place for bombs and weapons, and they ran security searches on the whole staff, and planned where to put marksmen on the roofs. It could have felt laborious or intrusive but instead it was a treat because they joked and teased us all so that no one could feel unduly stressed about the visit – we were in the hands of the professionals.

Matthew and his father, Peter Rice, planned a triumphal arch to span the narrow point of the yard through which we would all walk after the arrival when, along with the Lord Lieutenant in his unspeakably sexy uniform of tight trousers and spurs, we would form a receiving line. The arch was to be approximately 24 feet high and 16 feet wide; it was covered in white pottery and topped with a giant Prince of Wales insignia made out of cut paper sprayed with silver and adorned with many glass jewels. Peter is a theatre designer, still hard at work in his eighties and veteran of almost countless productions, but it was bitterly cold and he had been unwell; moreover, it seemed inevitable that it would rain. While Lizzy, Kitty, Margaret and I were having our hair done in Hanley in the morning, Matthew and Peter were out in the yard with our maintenance team and a tall scaffolding tower, screwing gallon teapots and plates onto the arch, and up in the studio the five-foot-tall paper Prince of Wales feathers were waiting to be installed at the very last minute.

Matt and I were to attend the Mayor's lunch, which was full of all sorts of colourful people – my favourite was the Staffordshire terrier mascot of the Mercian regiment. When we left for this, the arch looked far from finished and I was feeling anxious. Matt explained patiently and calmly that his father had never yet failed to be ready for a first night. And indeed, when we dashed back into the yard an hour later, just 10 minutes before the royal cars were due to arrive, all was – very nearly – ready. In a few minutes more the scaffold had disappeared and the feathers were still crisp, despite an icy drizzle. There was no time to worry, it was time to line up, and with a huge frisson of excitement we saw the flashing lights of the escort out on Lichfield Street, then the cars swept into the factory yard at dashing speed.

We curtsied and bowed and the first round of introductions was survived. I am really, really bad at names, so this was the only part I actually felt sick about; when I'm introducing people I get so nervous that I can't clearly remember my own name, and Matthew has yet to forgive me for once introducing him as Tim Rice. To be honest he is lucky it hasn't happened lots more. Then we walked under the arch, which was much admired – and it really was splendid; Peter is a wizard.

As we walked around the factory, the carefully planned tour went straight out of the window because the Prince was quite unwilling to bypass, as planned, several groups waving from outside the designated path. He went up to each group, smiling and asking funny, interested questions, and continued to do so as frantic signals were exchanged among his team. As a result, even the staunchest and most ruggedly independent-minded people in the factory that day were swept up in the happiness of the event. When the cars zoomed away we were all left smiling and hugging each other as if we were at a rave.

LITTLE ALTARS
EVERYWHERE

WE HAVE AN UNENDING PROBLEM. Both Matthew and I buy more china than any kitchen can hold. Every likely place has rows of extra jugs, plates, mugs, coffee pots. There was – is – continuously so much china in the house that it is silting up in boxes, in cupboards, and even spilling outside into the barn and sheds. We tried to call a halt to the shopping but it was no good, neither of us could pretend to be indifferent when passing a new junk shop or market. And besides, we realised that if we stopped feeling acquisitive about it, this had a negative effect on our designing; it seems to be a vital part of the creative process to keep one's eye in and keep shopping. Indifference to an antique shop, even if completely feigned, is reflected in stilted design and much less of a feeling of happy anticipation at sitting down to create anything new.

What could I do? Matthew drily suggested that I should stop buying children's books, especially as nobody much seems to read them. He was correct – that would free up an awful lot of shelf. But I often stop for a browse, in passing, when I can't resist a fix of *Just William*, or *Back in the Jug Agane*, or *Orlando the Marmalade Cat*. It is out of the question to stop buying children's books, old and new. Besides, I am sure that eventually a child will come along who loves books as much as I did in childhood. In the meantime I will keep on grouping choice editions of Kipling, Hull and Whitlock, Rosemary Sutcliff and Philippa Pearce, making librarian's selections beside beds, and putting sofas on tempting verandas in hope of summoning the bookworms. So the jugs and teapots slog it out with the Noel Streatfeilds and Elizabeth Goudges on the shelves. It's a continuous jostling bunfight.

One afternoon after a muddy day out on the marsh, we stopped at the house of an old friend of Mum's. The children were prompt to wash their muddy feet and legs and shed their filthy plimsolls, as Mary's standards are high and her teas legendary. Once they were all munching on home-made scones and jam around her kitchen table, we took our cups of tea next door into her lovely sitting room and flopped into her extra comfy sofas and chairs, being wary of sitting on her dog, as that too could be pretty strict. I told Mary that the children were loving their tea and how delicious it all was, and we fell to discussing proper cakes. She reminded me that Mum had had a particular fondness for parkin, and was once caught hiding behind the drawing room door at Scalbeck Hall, scoffing a whole plate of it while the other children played French and English – several bad crimes all at once. Greed: it's a family thing. I had forgotten about parkin though, and vowed to make it again very soon.

As we talked I noticed for the first time that the room had an elegant, narrow shelf running all around it, about 7 feet from the floor, above the picture rail. It was filled with Mary's collection of beautiful china, including a lovely dessert service with assorted hand-painted flowers and deep green borders, as well as copper lustre and other pretty things. She said that the china had belonged to her mother and she liked having it out of harm's way, well above grandchild level, and not in the kitchen where it was too likely to be put to use.

This was an idea to be adopted as widely as possible, and I rang the builder soon after and asked him to come and fit some china shelves. They were to be as slender and lightweight as possible, just 4 inches deep, with a groove routed along at the back of the shelf for plates to rest in so they would not slide off, and discreet brackets, as small as could be. I decided in the first instance that I did not want the shelves to be as high as Mary's; about 5 feet from the floor makes the china more visible, and besides, I want to be able to take pieces down fairly easily and frequently.

It started in a modest way. We had recently turned a small bedroom into an extra bathroom. It had an impractical but pleasing bath, set on a step under the window so that in daylight you could look out into the lime trees and keep an eye on the comings and goings. And the windowsill was handy for a book and a cup of tea, or occasionally a glass of wine. But at night, from now on, I envisaged lying in the bath admiring a collection of plates. We had decided to line the bathroom with tongue-and-groove boarding for cosiness, and Phil, the builder, suggested that the boarding might end at the shelf. This excellent suggestion was instantly adopted. The bathroom was soon finished and then painted. I chose a pale, slightly warm grey for the boarding and shelf, a pale sand colour for the walls above, and Marmoleum lino for the floor in a swirled grey and pale yellow.

The last and nicest job of all was to decide what china to put on the shelf. After not much deliberation, I decided that – taking my cue from Mary again – I would use it for our most fragile or formal china. I didn't think that there was very much of this, and I went around the house collecting together what I planned as a calm, well-spaced selection of mostly white porcelain and bone china, several pieces decorated with lustre, some hand-painted roses, a couple of intricate gold border designs and two Wedgwood creamware plates that I particularly love. There was sufficient depth, just, to add cups and saucers, with the saucers alternating along the wall with plates. One of our nicest wedding presents was a collection of small fragile cups and saucers in a mixture of patterns, like the china on the dresser in the kitchen of *The Tailor of Gloucester*. The result looked most satisfactory, and indeed it made me very happy while soaking in the bath. But the orderly look did not last long; as time went on I found more and more neglected pieces to join this collection, until the shelf was tight-packed. While I miss the sparse look, I'm resigned to a crowd, and in fact it is very useful to know where to look for formal and intricate designs, all in one place.

*

In 2006 we went to Portugal to investigate designing a porcelain range using a different mood, along the lines suggested by this bathroom china collection. We liked the factory found for us by an agent, near the coast between Nazaré and Alcobaça – so much so, in fact, that we sat down in the factory studio as soon as we arrived and completed the pattern of a charm bracelet there and then. The factory was custom-built when trade customers first migrated away from Stoke in the 1980s in search of cheaper prices, and perhaps also tempted by the thought of cold white wine and grilled fish on the beach as a vastly preferable working lunch to the produce from the chip van in Stoke.

The factory was a joy to work in, so light and spacious and, well, empty. For sadly the flighty merchandisers and commercial teams had moved on again pretty quickly, leaving the place almost high and dry. Charm Bracelet is still one of my very favourite designs, with hearts, crosses, anchors, cowboy hats, and even a wonderful death's-head hawkmoth charm on every piece in the tea-set because Michael found one in our garden that summer and it was so strange and beautiful that it had to be included in a design. The range had fetching packaging, but we had got it all wrong and our customers were completely foxed by our foray into white porcelain with a pink and gold design. It failed to sell, so we regretfully sold the stock on at a discount. I am still preoccupied by this theme; I think we will try again. But not just yet.

We went to nearby Alcobaça the next day, on our way back to the airport, and found the town's staggeringly wonderful monastery, which had quite the best plumbing of any kitchen anywhere – a fast-running stream ran right through the room, gushing through vast stone sinks.

As for shelves, well, this was just the beginning. After I realised how quickly I could fill a room with china – and how pleasing it is to be able to see it all without having to rootle about in the barn, going through boxes and disturbing nesting bantams – I asked Phil to put up shelves all through the house: over doorways; along passages; really just about anywhere there was some wall space free. The groupings evolve readily, as I find something nice in the factory or acquire a tea-set at a car boot sale or whatever. I like colour-based groups, and themes such as ware with writing on it. Matthew made lots of mugs and plates, particularly for Lizzy and Kitty, when the children were little. Many of these were flung about a bit and lack handles, or they have been glued together, so it's just as well they are out of the fray, as they are worth preserving, and sometimes offer reminders of nice ideas otherwise long forgotten.

Matt and I have a difference of opinion about arranging a house; he moves things around freely whereas I like to find a place for an object, and for that thing to stay put. This goes for all the furniture and pictures, as well as these shelves full of china. But alas, to Matthew, all furniture is only temporarily arranged and he is happy to use the kitchen table and chairs in a shop fit. In favour of frequent movement is the fact that he always surrounds his desk with a beautiful and inspiring arrangement of objects and images, adding to the tableau all the time, whilst always carrying to the next workplace a handful of totems which have passed safely through the storms of many house and studio moves. Some things, he claims, have been on his desk since he arrived at Bedales aged 13; so in fact he too has a strong feeling for continuity.

Things get dusty, but I like that time settles over the group, adding other elements – maybe a group of clay figures from India too fragile for much handling, or nice invitations, or letters, feathers or paintings. Eventually the group becomes a single entity with an increasing power to invoke memories, ideas and inspiration. Matthew likens these arrangements to an iconostasis in an orthodox church, saying that he is clear that these are no mere still lifes, but much-loved and cherished trophies in profound relationship to each other. I know what he means. It seems as if these shelf arrangements really are little altars to creative inspiration, whose regular contemplation is a fundamental part of making design.

SCONES WITH BUTTER
AND JAM

* * *

Makes approx. 24

Sift 450g self-raising flour, 4 teaspoons of baking powder and a pinch of salt into a mixing bowl or a food processor and rub in 100g chilled diced butter. Stir in 50g caster sugar. Beat 2 medium, free-range eggs together in a measuring jug, add 2 heaped tablespoons of soured cream and make up to 300ml with some creamy milk. Lightly mix most of the eggy mixture into the flour mixture, then knead very lightly and very briefly on a lightly floured surface until smooth. Roll out to a thickness of 2cm and using a small, maybe even heart-shaped cutter, cut into about 24 scones, re-kneading and rolling the trimmings two or three times. Place on lightly buttered baking trays, brush with the rest of the eggy mixture and bake at 220°C/200°C fan/gas 7 for 10–12 minutes until golden. Leave to cool, then split in half and serve spread with butter and home-made strawberry jam.

TRADITIONAL YORKSHIRE PARKIN

※ ※ ※

Line an 18cm (7 inch) deep, square cake tin with non-stick baking paper. Heat 200g black treacle, 100g dark muscovado sugar and 100g butter in a pan over a low heat, stirring until smooth. Cool slightly. Sift 100g plain flour, ½ teaspoon of baking powder, ¼ teaspoon of bicarbonate of soda, 2 teaspoons of ground ginger, 1 teaspoon of grated nutmeg and a large pinch of salt into a mixing bowl and stir in 200g medium oatmeal. Stir in the melted mixture with 150ml milk and 1 large egg, and beat until smooth. Pour into the tin and bake at 160°C/140°C fan/gas 3 for approximately 50 minutes until the cake is 'firmish' and a skewer comes away cleanly. Do not overcook it or it will become dry. Cool in the tin for 5 minutes, then transfer to a cooling rack and leave to go cold. Wrap in grease-proof paper, then foil, and store in an airtight tin for a couple of days before eating.

* * *

MATTHEW KNOWS A LOT
ABOUT CHICKENS

ON THE DAY we signed the lease on the farmhouse
in Worstead we had with us a crate of chickens
from Fulham, who were to take up residence a few days
before us. We left them in the car – it was a cool wintery
day – while we transacted our business with the landlord
and the agent inside the house. We wrangled fairly politely
over the details such as the state of the decor – 'like
Blenheim' said the owner. We eyed the exposed brickwork
and rugged timber table and benches in the kitchen,
which maybe, just maybe (and extremely indirectly),
owed distant inspiration to Graceland, and wondered
if this was true, then comforted ourselves with the unlikely
bonanza of heating in the greenhouse, not to mention

the nightclub in the cellar decorated with snow scenes and cobbled panels, and signed.

The house had four enormous bedrooms, a lovely Regency dining room, hall and drawing room, plus a kitchen (not from my dreams, but never mind), a play-room, an inhospitable garden room, an office, a boot room, a larder – and don't forget the pool and sauna, which had a rather battered sound system and party lighting. The whole house sported a 1970s finish which we came to feel extremely fond of, especially once we had painted throughout in deep colours and stapled red felt over the flock wallpaper in the drawing room. But none of these details mattered. The real draw for me was that we would be in Norfolk, and for Matthew it was the garden and the barns.

Once the paperwork was done we stepped outside and began our farewells. Suddenly the landlord stopped mid-sentence and stared open-mouthed at our car. We turned to follow his gaze. The chickens had broken out of the crate and were perched on the steering wheel and head rests, and we could now hear muffled crowing from the cockerels, clearly as keen as we were to get on with this exciting new venture.

One of the moot points in the lease had been the avail-ability of land beyond the garden. The landlord, a busi-nesslike farmer, sensibly didn't want to see the small paddocks around the house fill with docks and nettles, and suggested we should rent grazing as the need arose, doubting that Matthew really wanted his own sheep. He was right about the sheep, as it turned out. We did not have our own until after our next move, when the house came with a stockman in attendance. But Matthew was in need of more land than Gavin expected for poultry purposes, and so a small paddock beyond one of the lawns was to be included in the lease. We asked if we could explore and settle the chickens in after Gavin and Henry departed. With some surprise they agreed, then swished away in their large vehicles.

Matthew and I stood in the yard and just smiled and smiled, happy and slightly reeling at what we had just done.

Over the next six months we were both more often reeling than purely happy. The move had been swift: we quit Fulham for Norfolk within four months of the first conversation on the subject, leaving our house in London pretty much as it stood, to be lived in by a series of chefs from the River Café, overseen by fierce and devoted Gloria, who kept them all in order whilst cleaning and hoovering twice a week to hold back the tide of fag-ends and wine bottles.

Meanwhile three pantechnicons arrived in Worstead from Minety. It would have been just two but for an old

Oxford friend of Mum and Rick who arrived during the packing up at Minety, walked around the garden and pointed out the contents of the barns, stables and sheds, not to mention all the benches, rollers, chicken coops and so on lying in the bushes, which had not been taken into account. He left with the rhubarb forcers, and Rick, in his battered green van. Whilst amazed by the extras, I was grateful to him over and over again as we made the garden at Worstead. I soon got over some slight guilty twinges about leaving the Minety roses spread out on the lawn for the new owners – like Bobby Charlton's comb-over, as one of the removal men said – because it was so wonderful to plant the same New Dawns and Albertines in our first Norfolk kitchen garden on the familiar rose arches.

Cleaning, mending and redeploying the furniture from Minety to make a completely new life for us in Worstead had a bracing effect on me, like a strong pot of tea, and I was able to put behind me that melancholy haunted evening when we divided Mum's things. I hoped that she would be pleased, and knew that I could never know, and put that aside too.

Our friends in London were interested, appalled, affronted not to have been consulted, keen to be invited to stay and all other reactions in between. It sometimes felt at the beginning as if we'd taken too huge a step, but Matthew was good at ignoring the big issues and focusing on the details, which was usually comforting, and his first priority was to get a **lot** of chickens. The removal men declined to bring livestock, so I think Matthew must have caught up the Minety bantams and brought them himself. They were shut up for a week in a stable and thereafter fended for themselves, but always close by the house, which was the plan. They got used to breakfast on one small lawn on the east side of the house and lunch around on the sunnier side, always turning up to join in, hoping for scraps. I like the sight of bantams clustering over a child's discarded helping of spaghetti – they really get animated over it.

The rest of the chicken population, headed up by the occupants of our car on the first day, took up residence in a huge wooden shed in the extra paddock, as Matthew had had in mind from the start. He discovered the rump of the livestock market in Norwich on Saturday mornings and went regularly with the car full of cardboard boxes to transport his purchases home. He was tempted by goats. I was not. But he succumbed to almost every other possible purchase. We had ducks, who had to be given a child's plastic bath to swim in, but sometimes escaped into the garden and of course loved the swimming pool. And we had guinea fowl, turkeys, pigeons, doomed bunnies. . . and chickens and chickens and chickens, of every sort and description.

There was a rather sordid dog kennel, which our dogs hated and happily gave up, where Matthew housed a succession of cob chickens, who we all found it hard to have good feelings about, as their life plans were so brutally businesslike – it was a case of eat then be eaten for them. Once safely in the oven I can admit that they are as delicious, if fed a natural diet, as any poulet bought in a market in France, but they are depressing. Whereas the rest of the poultry world is full of pleasures and delights. That is, as long as it is managed by Matthew, who is knowledgeable, enthusiastic, unsqueamish, greedy, inspired, covetous, curious and unstoppable – about all sorts of things, but especially poultry. He seems to have kept chickens and other small caged beasts since childhood, regarding Chiswick then Fulham as perfect for the sport. Our neighbours, like those of his parents on Chiswick Mall, grew used to the sight of him armed with a landing net, flitting over the walls of the back gardens all down the street in pursuit of escapees. He proved that if they can't stretch up on their toes, the cockerels do indeed seem not to make too much noise, and the incentive of free eggs has often won around sceptics. Moreover, those eggs are so spectacularly delicious, such a simple vindication of very small-scale animal husbandry in their peerlessness in comparison to the shop-bought equivalents, that they are the best reasoning for keeping chickens. I agree with Matthew, everyone should do it. But they need a hotline to him for consultation on those disgusting matters of mites, scaly leg, egg binding and of course slaughter. . . So on the whole Waitrose probably does not need to panic yet.

Without him I would, I guess, do what Mum did – and most of her family still do, which is keep bantams. They are beautifully self-sufficient, and I would settle for fewer eggs, which I might have to hunt for high and low, rather than go in for intensive management. But it is just that intensity that Matt likes so much, and over the years he has dabbled enthusiastically in breeding programmes, rearing experiments, incubators mechanical and natural, and every culinary use of chicken and egg. Not to mention guinea fowl, ducks, geese and turkeys. . .

Unarguably a part of human life the world over, chickens – so homely and near at hand, so bountifully generous with their eggs, and so lovely to watch as they shepherd their chicks and teach them how to take a dust bath under a bay tree outside your kitchen window – have frequently proved inspiring, especially when it comes to the decoration of everyday wares. It is as if their char-acters, lifestyles and ultimate destinations all combine to speak of kitchen china, and from ancient times poultry often and often scrambles and struts around kitchen plates and jugs and bowls in decorative poses. Matthew would happily draw them all day long, and luckily he sometimes does. His chicken designs on Emma Bridgewater pottery are always popular and it's easy to see why.

CHICKEN PIE

✳ ✳ ✳

Put a 2kg (preferably free-range) chicken in a large pan with 2 peeled and halved onions, 3 peeled cloves of garlic, ½ teaspoon of black peppercorns, 1 teaspoon of salt, a large sliced carrot and a halved lemon. Cover with water, bring to the boil, then leave to simmer for 40 minutes. Turn off the heat and leave the chicken in the liquid until cool enough to handle. Remove the meat from the bones, discarding the skin and bones, and break it into small, chunky pieces. In a 1.75–2 litre pie dish, combine the chicken meat, a bunch of trimmed and finely chopped spring onions, and 50g pine nuts fried in a little butter until golden. Boil the chicken stock rapidly until reduced to 900ml, then strain into a jug. Melt 75g butter, stir in 75g plain flour, cook a few seconds then gradually stir in the stock. Simmer for 5 minutes. Stir in up to 100ml double cream if you wish, season to taste and pour over the chicken to nearly fill the dish. Push a pie bird into the centre of the filling and leave to go cold. For the pastry, rub 90g chilled butter and 90g chilled lard into 350g plain flour sifted with ½ teaspoon of salt. Stir in 3–4 tablespoons of cold water to make a soft dough. Knead briefly, then use to cover the top of the pie. Decorate with some pastry leaves made from the trimmings, glaze with beaten egg, and cook in a medium oven set at 180°C/160°C fan/gas 4 for 45–50 minutes or until golden brown and bubbling hot.

A JAR OF MUSTARD AND
A BOX OF MATCHES

THE PARTNERSHIP between Matthew and Marcus and myself, formed shortly after Matt and I were married, was the power base that established our business. In the end the partnership was wound up, but along the way there were some really good times. A friend said that she saw us in the Fulham Road: I was wearing a bright red embroidered Afghan robe and swinging along, laughing, between Marcus and Matthew. As it happens, I think that on that day we were on our way to the bank to formalise a loan to stock a shop in Paris. Catherine said that our partnership looked like full-time fun. And it was.

We all three had always loved the idea of building

up business in France, and so we used to set up our stand in a trade fair (so much more evocatively known in France as a salon) in Paris twice a year for some five years and opened about 50 good accounts. We grappled with disdainful Parisian fashionistas who smoked furiously and dropped ash in the samples, and charming Frenchmen, often impressively unabashed to be doing business attended by a poodle on a lead. We delighted in the many contrasts to the halls of the NEC in Birmingham, where the equivalent event holds no such characters and seems principally to be a shrine to hygiene, health and safety, where dogs large or small could in no stretch of the imagination participate. In Paris we ate lots of delicious suppers all over the city – and picnics on our stand – and generally enjoyed ourselves so much that we decided to open a shop there. It was a simple deal whereby we renamed the shop of an existing stockist in the rue Daubenton, close to the Botanic Garden, the Great Mosque and the Sorbonne in the 5th arrondissement. Best of all, it was just around the corner from the run down, but still wonderful street market in the rue Mouffetard. Our partner-to-be was doing good business, we thought, so at her invitation we simply built some new shelves, painted our name over the door and filled it with stock of the latest designs.

It didn't work out, and just a few months later we tidied up, closed the door and drove away. The net loss was small, but we set against this the pleasure of getting to know a new part of Paris and that was that.

For me this was simply another bead strung on pretty much my favourite necklace. Mum and Pop used to meet, I think secretly, on the Left Bank during the 1950s before they married. Both spoke of the city with that welling up of remembered happiness that said so much more than the actual proffered accounts of how they spent their time. Pop was working for his mother's family firm, an engineering business in Wakefield; he had been sent to learn the ropes in a French foundry. As a result he speaks admirably idiomatic French, in contrast to Mum's schoolgirl style, which she acquired along with several other debutantes staying *en pension* with a respectable lady who was to give the girls a little conversational French. Certainly Mum learnt to make especially delicious omelettes in a heavy French cast iron pan, which may have been more use in the long run. My parents came home and got engaged, and I only ever went to France as a child with one or the other of them, after they parted, so I like to think that the homecoming feeling I get in the Latin Quarter goes back directly to them wandering there, young and in love.

✳

When coming home from a holiday in France, in the hour or two before driving onto the ferry, Mum always went shopping. Of course she bought baguettes, pains au chocolat, some pâté and a cheese (all of which were harder to come by in Oxford in the 1970s than they are now), but her especial pleasure was to buy everyday groceries – tins of flageolets, a jar of confit, a packet of lentils, oil, vinegar, salt, coffee, a jar of mustard and a box of matches. She said that this prolonged the pleasure of being in France a bit longer and gave her a small Gallic thrill when she lit the gas or made a salad dressing. Now it is necessary to seek out perhaps a rather dingy shop – a regional supermarket can yield a good result – and scope the shelves carefully for brands that are not exported widely to gain the same effect, but I always do this, and it gives me quite disproportionate pleasure. Matthew used to take this idea to extreme lengths, culminating in a chick and duckling smuggling exercise which gave me such palpitations (there was audible cheeping and quacking as we approached the customs, so Matthew instructed the children to make animal noises to cover them) that he promised to keep his shopping legal in future.

Matthew and I married in December 1987, and our honeymoon in Urbino was not an auspicious start to our married life – the city was closing for the holidays and the palpable feeling of winter, absence, emptiness, closed doors and empty streets was not a good setting. When he proposed four months earlier, in a kitchen garden, we had been going out together for just ten weeks, so it's fair to say that we simply didn't know each other well enough in Urbino to access the confidence in odd pleasures that only really comes from a strong bond. But Matthew has always been a man of resource and, realising that a change of plan was urgently needed, he rang a friend in Florence, just catching him as he was about to leave the family's flat in the city to go home to England for Christmas. Matt's anguished squeak of relief – Poldy! – was met with surprise and interest, and once he had clarified that this was not his granny but Matthew, Leopold and his friends agreed to wait to let us into the flat so we could spend five days there. In the event they stayed on, thinking that a honeymoon would make good spectator sport. Leopold and his friends were nearly ten years younger than us and their company was so funny that they saved us from disaster; we had a lovely time in Florence and have yet to go back to Urbino.

In spring 1988 we went to Normandy and in three days created the template for our foreign holidays for the next few years. We were both working hard – still on separate businesses at this point – thus, then as now, time was of the essence. So how to get maximum benefit? And how to get home feeling as if you have had a holiday, rather than an ordeal? The answers we established are: that we go abroad, but not too far away; if we drive, we can shop; and (to set against this) if we fly, we travel very light, never checking in our bags on the way out at least, so we can manage to carry quite a bit of hardware home with us. This first trip to Normandy was by car, and we found atmospheric cheap hotels, restaurants with a penchant for slamming the kitchen door at 1.45pm (from which we quickly learnt not to dither over restaurant choices) and spectacular cooking. And maybe better still, we found markets for picnic shopping, and fields and beaches providing matchless picnic spots, and lovely walking and swimming. So we bought a squashy basket, two glasses, a knife, a corkscrew and a couple of cloths as our basic picnic kit, and delved into that eternally infuriating question – why the hell are the French so much better than the Brits at food? – as we scoffed our way happily through a big and unscientific research programme.

If you take the trouble, and it is a bit of a faff, it is perfectly possible to make utterly delicious pâtés at home. Matthew's mother has periodic crazes for this and the results are jolly exciting. But if you are French there is no need, as you are spoilt for choice, with terrines, rillettes, parfaits and pâtés of every description to buy from countless *boucheries*, market stalls and vans; meanwhile we seem not to have progressed far beyond potted meat / fish paste – delete whichever it tastes least like and savour the thought that the principal ingredient of either type might be coot, at least it was when the big shoots in east Norfolk still went in for mass waterfowl slaughter. I admit that we are fast improving and while our regional cheeses may not manage to compete on equal terms with those of Normandy, we have rediscovered our pride and we now do some fantastic things with milk, even if too much of the output of our beleaguered dairy farms ends up in an industrial product. I have to confess that I find it hard to completely kick the squeezy cheese habit on Norfolk picnics, but I'd rather buy cheese anywhere in France than anywhere in Britain, so it's still France *douze points*, and Grand Bretagne – let's be generous and say *un point*, in the Eurovision cheese contest.

Bread? Ah, this is a game of two halves: no bread-related experience can ever truly be more heavenly than strolling to the *boulangerie* to buy baguettes early in the morning – and we are slavishly adopting French sourdough, inspired by Poilâne, as part of urban life – but I will always love to come home to make three fat spelt loaves in the Aga.

What about biscuits? We can thrash the Frogs on this small but not completely unimportant issue, for who wants a dry galette when they can have a Jaffa cake? And when it comes to confiture, well, they try but they just don't really get it, I think because French jam has far too much sugar in it, every time! And their sweets are hopeless. So when it comes to a little something to go with your peach, a piece of chocolate, say, you are at a loss when picnic shopping in France. This may be why they are less fat than us as a nation. That and the Gauloises – one of the girls in our office says she is sometimes berated by her French granny:

Mais Sarah, tu es tout à fait grosse! Prends une cigarette, ma petite.

Whereas Pop's mother, known to us as Kelburn Granny, shared that enthusiasm for smoking, she had little or no passion for food or kitchens. I can only just picture the basement kitchen in Cheyne Walk where a Portuguese couple toiled. I think perhaps I only went there once. In fact we would be more likely to totter round the corner from their front door to the Santa Croce restaurant to toy with a slice or two of beef carpaccio, between cigarillos, than eat at home. Meanwhile Mum's mother, known simply as Granny, knew that she ought to love her kitchen, and working in it, because she was enraptured like everyone else by Elizabeth David's ground-breaking and instantly-classic cookbook, *French Provincial Cooking*.

From the 1950s onwards Granny frequently packed her brown Revelation suitcase and trotted through Pimlico to the BOAC building to nip to France or Italy. And she made intrepid trips by bus all over mainland Greece, developing an early taste for yoghurt and honey, and aubergines, and courgettes cooked in olive oil with garlic and oregano. So Granny bought all the rest of her books and went to the Elizabeth David shop in Bourne Street to buy lovely French cooking equipment, but the reality always disappointed her. She tried to cure her fear of ovens with a timer and a thermometer, but each meal was shadowed slightly by the tensions involved in making it, and the more we weighed, measured and timed, the more wayward the results, and the more harried the cook and her assistant.

I still have her battered copy of *French Provincial Cooking* and I am well aware that it is the backbone of any good food I ever produce. One of my favourite recipes is for gougère. It's years since I actually referred to the recipe, so this one may not be as it is writ there, but this works really well and it's a nice supper to have on a Sunday night with a green salad and an episode of *Downton Abbey*.

GOUGÈRE

***

Chop 75g butter into small pieces and drop into 300ml milk with some salt and black pepper. Bring to the boil. Away from the stove, add 125g plain flour (sifted) all in one go. Beat vigorously until it becomes a smooth shiny paste which comes away from the sides of the pan. Add 4 medium eggs, one at a time, beating hard throughout. Now add lots of cheese, coarsely grated. I use Gruyère, Cheddar or Parmesan, or a mixture. Whereas you have to be careful with the choux paste, you can be really generous with the cheese – up to 100g. I also add 2 teaspoons of Dijon or English mustard. Stir in the cheese, keeping a handful to sprinkle on top. Butter a large baking sheet and draw a circle with your fingertip about 12–13cm in diameter. Then, using a dessertspoon, arrange spoonfuls of the paste (like meringues) round the circle. Repeat this process, laying the next lot on top of the first, bridging the gaps between them. Paint the paste ring with a little beaten egg, sprinkle with the remaining cheese and put the baking sheet in a preheated oven at 220°C/200°C fan/gas 7. After 10 minutes reduce the heat to 190°C/170°C fan/ gas 5, and continue cooking for another 30–35 minutes. Watch out – it looks done before it is and is liable to collapse if removed from the oven prematurely. Eat immediately! This might be a starter, or a meal on its own as a light lunch or supper, and is especially good with a green salad.

FRIDAY NIGHT AT
MINETY

IT'S A FRIDAY NIGHT in late October. Alex and I had left London later than we meant to, so it's after eight when we arrive in Minety. I love the moment when he turns off the car engine and silence falls deafeningly when Carly Simon is interrupted. He flicks off the headlights and, as my eyes adjust, it's dark and starry in the drive, all the lights are on and the house shines out, sailing through the velvety night. I get out, stand and stretch and look at it, and love the idea of so much life contained inside. As I think this, one of my little sisters dashes across the playroom window, followed by the other. Mum says that this is her favourite view of the house: from the stables (which are just behind me, about 50 yards from the house) at night; with the cosy smell of the horses and the sounds of them munching, shifting and stamping; and the house an Atkinson Grimshaw painting across the garden.

When I think of this later I understand that the pleasure is to do with the way that, as a mother, you strain your every fibre to make your family happy; to make a home, a garden, and all of that, and by the way to have supper ready; and that this makes you proud, and constantly preoccupied. But mostly it just keeps you always busy, so busy that you rarely stop to think about any of it. And so it is, that you especially love the moments when you are still in the whirl of it – as Mum would have been at that moment, checking the girls' ponies after hunting – and yet for an instant you are outside it and so you are briefly able to see it from a distance, and you can almost understand what you have made. Almost. It's like catching a glimpse of yourself unexpectedly in full profile as a mirror swings in a shop changing room, but much bigger.

Alex has a box of pottery in his arms.

Shall we leave everything else for the moment?

I'll just get the queer gear from Covent Garden. Rick will like that.

We had been to the market at 5.30pm, just catching the

tail-end of trading, to buy armfuls of flowers for a shoot for the photographer who Alex still assisted from time to time when he didn't have enough work on. And we had lucked-in with a veg stall just finishing up and grudgingly prepared to sell us an exotic mix of leftover chillies, lemons, salads, peppers, bunches of herbs and suchlike for a tenner.

So, bearing boxes, we push open the boot room door, then the door into the map-lined passage, and finally the kitchen door at the end – always a slight struggle since Rick's obsession with draughts and slamming doors had led him to put door closers on all the doors into this, the busiest room, and the kitchen one was especially strong. Mum is stirring something on the Aga, Rick is putting new candles in the slightly crooked black chandelier that hangs over the table, frequently spattering multicoloured wax into the salt below. From under the side-table beside the stove, the collie Midge looks up and woofs and smiles and wags her tail.

Darling. Darlings – Alex, how lovely. Supper will be ready very soon. Veg, oh what a relief. I need chives to snip onto the chowder. Thank you.

Alex was extremely domesticated, so Mum loved his visits – she was usually more than happy to delegate cooking chores. Being nine years older than me, he sort of stopped being anything to do with me at home and would happily spend the weekend mending a mower with Rick or something.

Alex is already quizzing Mum about how she had made the chowder. I have put the recipe at the end of the chapter in case you would like it. I have found, in the passing devout stages when fish on Friday seems important, or just when I happen to find a half-decent fishmonger, that this dish is very popular, not being too overtly fishy, and it will hang about if some are late, and it's easy to stretch if numbers vary. So what's not to like?

✳

Em, I didn't know you were here.

My youngest sister Clover comes into the kitchen from the playroom holding her cat, Tibby.

Doesn't Tibby look sweet in this baby dress, Ems? I think she really likes it. Listen to her purring.

Indeed she is rumbling like an engine, for Tibby has been tamed and tickled into complete submission under Clover's imperial hand, just like any pony that Clover jumps onto. Tibby knows she has met her match and co-operates with whatever the project might be. She spends quite a lot of time in an old pram. And she really does look sweet in lace and ribbons. On other occasions, when I meet Tibby out of doors amongst the barns, I can only feel that, in her fierce rat controls, she is reasserting her wildness and independence. She is certainly deadly to rodents anyway. When not wearing a christening dress.

Have you brought anything with you? Clover glances into the box of veg. *Huh. Boring. What's in here?*

Why don't you put Tibby on the sofa and come and unwrap with me? I've got some samples of the pottery.

Nell, Nell, you've got to come – Emma's got pottery!

She shouts up towards the bedroom she and Nell share above the kitchen. Nell emerges from the doorway to the back stairs. She is slim and tall with a deep voice and hair cut short, like Nancy in *Swallows and Amazons*. This boyishness is accentuated by her clothes because she almost always wears boys' Aertex shirts and jeans, or shorts in summer, invariably with an ancient leather belt and a knife attached.

Together we unwrap the pottery, and Clover's squeaks and Nell's quiet remarks confirm what I am already silently completely sure of: that the pottery works. It looks real. We take it seriously. It isn't bungling and pretend – it is going to sell. Once I've worked on the designs a bit, as these are still very rudimentary, and the colours have not all worked: some are much too washed out, and a few really not right. These I 'disappear' along with the paper and the box, out of the back door, so we only have the good and almost-good ones left on the table.

Rick has been out of the kitchen to put more logs on the fire in the drawing room, and now he is back and opening a bottle of wine.

Ah, Ems, how's it going? Has anyone died from eating your food yet?

Kate has a job in a framer now, we're not doing the catering any more, and no, no one died. But thanks for asking. What do you think of the pots?

Charming, charming. Clearly the work of a complete amateur. Ho ho.

Oh Rick! Ignore him. They are lovely, darling. What is this one? I can't tell. Is it a shell . . . no, it's a daisy, isn't it? Lovely. Now, can you put it all on the dresser and lay the table? Supper's ready.

Ems, this is my favourite one – it's a fox, isn't it? It looks a little bit as if it's wearing flares, I like that.

Well, you must keep that one, sweetie.

Meanwhile Nell is being kind about a pattern of monkeys, which are her very favourite animal of all. I apologise for the place where the colour has run.

Oh, I don't mind the dribbly leg. It's fine if you turn it round this way.

Thank you darling. Keep it if you like. Don't ever let Rick use it, OK?

FISH CHOWDER

* * *

Poach 600g fish fillets (maybe a mixture of cod, ling and smoked haddock) in 600ml milk with some black peppercorns, blade mace and bay leaves for 2 minutes, then cover and set aside for 5 minutes. Lift the fish onto a plate to cool slightly and strain the milk into a jug. Flake the fish, discarding the skin and any bones. Boil 600g small, peeled potato chunks (floury ones) in salted water for about 15 minutes until tender. Drain and set aside. In a casserole dish, soften 250g chopped shallots in 2 tablespoons of olive oil with 100g chopped streaky bacon for 10 minutes (add a pinch of chilli flakes and/or about 1 teaspoon of lightly crushed fennel seeds for variety). Add the flaked fish and boiled potatoes to the casserole dish with 150ml cream, most of the milk from poaching the fish, 30g butter, lots of chopped parsley (or some chopped summer savory) and ground black pepper, and mix to combine without smashing them up too much. This will keep warm happily in the bottom left oven of the Aga until everyone gets home.

THE RAGGLE TAGGLE
GYPSIES-O

A T LUNCH ONE DAY a friend called Andrew surprised and horrified me by saying that a career starts at 14. For heaven's sakes, that is when a child chooses their GCSEs. I was appalled.

How can you know – or even have a clue – at that stage, what you want to do in life?

Precisely! he crowed. *Those choices matter, they start on the process of defining you.*

What he said made me realise that I had probably been doing all I could to avoid defining myself at school, and I was definitely still in the same frame of mind at university. And after. Some of the girls at school with me knew their paths from early on: they would inevitably follow their parents – into medicine probably, it was that sort of school. I think I was always envious, as I longed for my vocation to be revealed to me, perhaps in a dream, or while I ran around the track on the school playing-field reaching after that amazing flying feeling you sometimes get while you run. But mostly I was reluctant to commit; I think that in my teens I unconsciously wanted to be many things, and hated to have to choose. In my head I was variously a warrior queen, a waitress in a cool diner, a lady writer, a singer in a band, a social worker, a great runner. . .

Like a boyfriend from the time, I had difficulty squaring up to any real or likely role. In fact while I was at university, reading English Literature (where Anglo-Saxon and Middle English poetry were mandatory elements in the course, chosen to make it clear that I did not want to talk about the future), I took to using the answer he once came up with to that most-intrusive question so frequently put to young people: *What do you plan to do after university?*

When fending off this unacceptable nosiness, I murmured that I might like to choose which paintings to reproduce on the covers of paperback novels. And privately I aspired no further than typing the letters for whoever did this attractive-sounding job, in a muddly, fusty publisher's office, preferably in a raffish street in Soho.

✳

Andrew followed up his pronouncement about careers commencing at 14 with what I thought was a bit of a low blow. He said,

You know we can't encourage our children to go about their careers as if they were guerrilla fighters, like you do, Em.

Because in fact I had, without knowing it, been hatching a plan whilst apparently looking the other way, making my father anxious and my mum, who didn't care about my career (she minded far more about character, good humour and resourcefulness), mostly annoyed that I was out too much and not working hard enough. I know now that those apparently inactive phases are vital for decision-making. As long as I am brooding just consciously upon a dilemma, I can trust my subconscious to work away at it while I concentrate on, say, driving, or washing up, or hanging out the washing – any consuming but creatively undemanding activity will do. The answers will surface, as long as on some level somewhere you really want them to. I had a deep (invisibly deep, it might have been said) desire to be independent. Somehow I could see very clearly that I only had a very few years between finals and family life. I was pretty sure I'd marry swiftly and have lots of children, and I wanted to make my mark before that happened, despite having absolutely no idea as what. So plenty of subterranean trawling was going on. I was hugely aware of the question: *What shall I do? Or be?*

I knew I had energy, power even. I did not yet know where to direct it; but on some level I also felt pretty sure that a project would reveal itself to me.

More mystic than guerrilla fighter, surely?

✳

However, I admit that Andrew was perfectly fair in his assessment, in an intuitive way. Mum was simultaneously conventional and lawless, and she passed to all her children some elements of both. On long car drives we used to play the usual games, such as I Spy and Pub Cricket and I Went to Market, then when they lost their charm, we sang. Mum had a repertoire of songs that would take us all the way from Oxford to Norfolk. She loved traditional songs and ballads, hymns and marching songs, such as 'One is One and All Alone', 'Shenandoah', 'Barbara Allen', 'The British Grenadiers'. When Rick was assistant director in a production of *The Threepenny Opera*, Tom and I learnt 'Mac the Knife' and 'The Pirate Ship'. Then the musical *The Boyfriend* gripped us, along with *Joseph*, *Jesus Christ Superstar* and *Hair*, and we knew almost all of the songs from them by heart. But the song I identify most with Mum, that I can hear her singing most often, was 'The Raggle Taggle Gypsies'.

And I knew it wasn't just the tune she returned to; I assumed without thinking about it that she was, in a dreamy unfocused way, one and the same as the lady who left her fine house, beautiful dresses, linen sheets and newly-wedded lord for a romantic, runaway love affair. She made it clear that only dull, unimaginative people disapprove of gypsies, and made sure we were polite to the (in truth, scary) gypsy children when they came to the village school with us in Bassingbourn, while they and their families were camping on Watling Street to do the pea or sprout picking. And later, when there were gypsies camped on the verges around Cirencester, she would buy bags full of honey buns from Pam's Pantry in the market place and stop and give them to the children on her way home. Somehow she embodied a polite, unspoken, but insistent scepticism about convention. For example she had an effective charm when the police inevitably came to investigate her many parties. I picture her completely composed, smiling and joking, pressing chocolate cake and raspberries on them as the policemen clocked the drunken teenagers blundering into the furniture, and sniffed questioningly. They always left cheerily, having realised that she held the party in the palm of her hand; she was completely relaxed, and completely aware, without asking what we were all up to. Somehow she made us all feel that the eye of the storm was the safe place, and that we were going to make mistakes, surely; equally we were going to have to put everything right again afterwards.

Of course I remember all her parties swirled together

as a romantic whirlwind of music and dresses, of kisses, gold shoes, Rive Gauche, bowls of cherries, and lilies and roses. I know that it was not just me who recalled them this way: I remember the melancholy departure, after one long and lovely weekend, of a friend who said his thank yous, kissed me again on the doorstep and asked,

But I don't know where this is, how will I ever find my way back here?

Then he wandered away down the road pushing his bike. I knew what he meant: he was alluding to *Le Grand Meaulnes*, one of my favourite novels. Mum's parties had fugitive magic.

Quiet Nell. She is full of extraordinary inspiration. Two weeks after her Finals she got her first job in a circus, then over the next two years she worked for several different outfits, living in a caravan, riding an elephant, making popcorn, selling tickets and wielding a sledge-hammer. She graduated to ring mistress in a little French circus touring along the south coast, and then she went on to do a high school horse act in a big fancy circus in Germany. She met and married her perfect match; Toti Gifford is the most competent man in England, with a fleet of diggers and trucks, a theodolite in his head, a real gift for landscaping, plus a taste for adventure and back-breaking work to match Nell's. And a heart of gold.

Together they bought a tent and started Giffords Circus, a fantasy of what the world might be like if we were all to run away and live for art and adventure. The show is new every year. It is bold, imaginative and picturesque in the extreme, conjuring rare magic on village greens, sprinkling sequins and making such sweet music and visions of delight.

In one of the shows she curvetted around the ring on a black and white horse, dressed as a psychedelic gypsy cowgirl, while the band played 'Thank You for the Days'. Mum loved The Kinks and it was as if Nell conjured her up and paid thanks, then she and her horse bowed in tribute. And disappeared overnight. For in the morning there was nothing to say the circus had ever been pitched among the chestnut trees; the tent, the horses, the artistes and all the wagons had vanished, leaving only a sprinkling of sawdust in the worn grass.

So, it's clear that Mum was low on conventional careers advice. But it's not strictly fair to make it seem as if she didn't occasionally drift towards the subject – for example she had a phase of badgering me to be a midwife. This was directly linked to having had a wonderful experience when Nell and Clover were born, but I didn't realise until my own babies arrived that radical midwifery probably had played a big role; I could simply see that she was radiantly happy. Rather stupidly I didn't make the connection, couldn't see myself fitting into the environment of a hospital – radical or conventional – and discounted her suggestion on the grounds that even thinking about the circulation of the blood makes me faint. Her ideas about our careers were a long way from Andrew's conviction that 'It all begins at 14', that is for sure. Yet she made the world seem always full of wonderful possibility. And she gave all her children the conviction that we were going to be happy, and competent. And maybe not bound by expectations, but instead free to run away with the Raggle Taggle Gypsies, whatever we took that to mean.

LIFE IS A
PATCHWORK QUILT

MRS SPAIN TAUGHT US how to use a Singer sewing machine in the prehistoric days when all girls were taught Home Economics for a couple of years in the junior school, after which we made a shirt, then a simple dress, under her vigilant eye. I absolutely loved the project each time, but knew perfectly well that the results were not flattering garments – in fact they were impossible to wear. So I showered Mum and Granny with variations on an evening bag. Mum was kind enough to use hers. I remember her going out to dinner carrying a recently completed mushroom grey needlecord number with her lipstick, cigarettes and car keys in it. But the challenge was to think of something to make which was really worth having, and my eyes turned to Granny's huge patchwork quilt. It rustled with paper, as she insisted that writing paper was the very best weight for tacking the patches into shape, and she said that you could not take out the paper until the quilt was complete, which this one was, eventually, many decades after she started it. She brought it with her to work on when she came to stay when Nell and then Clover were born, and I was filled with ambition. Granny had no intention of letting me spoil her work with clumsy stitching. She was a top seamstress. I found it hard to believe that the tiny new-baby clothes that our teddies wore had been made by her for Mum and her brother and sister, Martin and Teesa, as babies; the stitches were fairy small. And since before I was born she had been making a carpet on a huge frame, worryingly reminding me of the Lady of Shalott and her curse. Moreover, she embroidered beautifully and knitted the best jerseys, as well as finding crochet easy. She was probably not unusually accomplished for her generation, but to me these were towering achievements – still are.

Instead Granny encouraged me to make a cushion, which was sensible, as I began and finished it while she was staying, and she pressed me to go to Gordon Thoday (oh, the lost haberdashers of old-fashioned high streets, how I miss them) to buy stuffing. It was all very pleasing. It was around the same time, in the early 1970s, that Laura Ashley opened a shop in Little Clarendon Street in Oxford, and it was instantly Mecca; the girls who worked there were almost as fascinatingly grown-up and glamorous as the waitresses in Browns, the recently opened and highly desirable hamburger restaurant full of potted plants and big mirrors just around the corner in St Giles. My friends and I yearned for all of the Laura Ashley dresses and spent ages trying to decide which pattern we would have. I chose a brown design for the dress I was to wear to Miranda's sixteenth birthday party. I feel a bit sad thinking about my 14-year-old self choosing such a drab colour. I guess it was because I have always been floored by choice, finding few situations more baffling than an empty car park – I just go round and round until someone else loses patience and says, *Park* right there – so perhaps Caroline or Lucy or Ginny looked up from dreams of raspberry pink, golden yellow and sea green and said vaguely, *Oh yes, that's really nice*, and I was relieved not to have to think about it any further.

The party was exciting because Miranda's mum, Felicity, had hired a jukebox for the evening and you could choose and key in the records. Actually some older boys staked it out to make sure that we danced only rock and roll; they were disgusted when we rushed at them and pushed in to put on 'Leader of the Pack' and

'Locomotion', but most of the evening was dominated by Jerry Lee Lewis and Elvis. I remember finding the dancing extremely nervous-making, then working on a frenetic skipping technique which I was quite taken with, only to be told by Miranda (whose dancing was assured) that it was OK but better not to move around so much, after which I felt less keen on it.

But the best thing about buying offcuts for making patchwork was that you could take lots of patterns and colours home, and I always did, and made several cushions.

Granny's quilt had some patches from shirts and dresses that she could remember; this was the thing about a real patchwork quilt which completely wound me in. I was in love with the idea that a bedspread could incorporate memories, people, favourite clothes long past wearing, aprons, baby clothes, even tablecloth fragments, present at so many feasts before becoming witness to your dreams. So when Clover had a son in 2000, I set about making him a quilt which incorporated, amongst other things, patches from a dress that Clover wore as a little girl and a dress from Annabelinda in Oxford that we could all remember as Mum's best dress, which she wore with pink suede boots, a big felt hat and a gorgeous emerald brooch shaped like a bow. I used a Penguin paperback as my template and decorated some of the patches with appliqué motifs – such as Jimmy Joe's initials, a lariat, hearts, hands, an elephant and a pair of ponies – before sewing the patches together and making a backing from an early Emma Bridgewater textile, sandwiching a layer of wadding between the two and stitching them together. I bought the wadding from John Lewis, which is less exciting than the old haberdashery stores but very reliable for sewing supplies now that almost all of the independent shops selling winceyette nighties, vast pants, felt squares and all possible sewing requisites over a wide mahogany counter have turned into Costa coffee shops.

This first project was both an act of love and a vastly satisfactory antidote to the stress of reclaiming the business, which was going on at the same time. I did all the sewing by hand, mostly because I just love doing it, but also because it meant that I could cuddle up on the sofa with the children and watch films. *The Commitments*, *The Talented Mr Ripley*, *Primary Colors*, *Strictly Ballroom*, *The Graduate*, *St Trinian's*, *The Coal Miner's Daughter* and *A Man for All Seasons* are all woven into this and the next few quilts I made. After Jimmy's, I made quilts for several other nephews and nieces, and I think by the time I made one for Clover's daughter Dolly I was getting more ambitious. Whilst driving across the Midwest with the girls, we discovered Walmart. The ostensible reason for our first visit was to get Matt's 35mm films developed on the spot, but there were so many enticing reasons to linger! The girls were lost in a heaven of terrible shoes and locked into the search for a match for the tee-shirt we saw on a wonderfully furious daughter in a diner one morning which shouted 'I (heart) my bad attitude' at her long-suffering family; Matthew was thrilled by the racks and racks of weapons; and I discovered the inspiring fact that in rural America craft skills, especially sewing, are alive and kicking – the dressmaking fabric selections were breathtaking, and I did not hold back. I chose lots of red-white-and-blue patterns with Western motifs including stars, guitars, boots, hats and bandanas, which all spoke to me of Clover's madly romantic year in Texas. I patched them together in big squares and appliquéd all across them 'I Love Dolly and Elvis', and felt huge pleasure in the result.

Next I made a bedcover for Mum using her aprons, tablecloths, shirts and so on. The message on it, appliquéd in blue felt, is 'I Love You More Than Mars Bars and Fish and Chips in the Rain'. It has been subject to fierce hot washing, and is now very faded and rather falling to pieces; I'm mending it so it can go back on her bed, but maybe it's a bit too sad. She is the only person I know who wants to eat two whole Mars bars. And the fish and chips part of the message alludes to a day when a picnic at Minster Lovell was rained off so she bought us all fish and chips in Witney, which we ate greasily in the car. Then when they were finished, she suddenly wound down all the windows of the car and said, *Quick, throw* all *the remains, yes,* and *the paper, out of the windows* now! – which surprising command we were delighted to obey, whilst indignant passing cars flashed and hooted. *Biodegradable*, she said, unconcerned, but the sheer naughtiness of the moment was dramatic. Normally we were forbidden to throw anything more than an apple core out of the car window.

At some point Matthew, who had been amused by my weekend spiritual migration from boardroom to *Little House on the Prairie*, said it was time I made quilts for our children. So at around the time we left Norfolk in 2008, I found a very washed-out old cotton quilt, faded to white but still sound, to use as backing to make a quilt for Margaret. Then I made a patchwork using about 240 patches from a four-inch-square template (cut from the estate agent's details of a farm inside the Oxford ring road that we were very taken with for a while), piecing together pinkish-coloured patterns, all cut from scraps that I had been half-consciously keeping for this very project. I used pieces from Matt's favourite Provençal shirts, a summer skirt of mine, one of Pat's design strike-offs, some rose-covered trousers given to Margy by a much-loved godmother, Mum's purple and white bathing sarong, and many others – all emotive as well as pretty things. I cut out the felt letters to spell Keep Very Cosy Darling Margaret, beautifully drawn by Matthew, and appliquéd them across the patchwork, as for Dolly's quilt. When this was done I sewed the patchwork onto a larger piece of an Emma Bridgewater textile, then sewed the sandwich onto the faded white piece and bound the edges with a mixture of favourite scraps to make a contrasting border. As with the earlier projects, I look at this now and hear the soundtrack to a bunch of favoured films – *Coyote Ugly*, *Almost Famous*, *Still Crazy*, *Stage Beauty* and others which I heard but barely saw as I sewed.

Margaret has always been the one in the family for making cakes. The recipe she turns to most often is probably Nigella's brownies – in fact I know she knows it by heart, she makes them so frequently – but she is also a confident experimenter with variations on a sponge cake; maybe throwing in a handful of redcurrants before baking the mixture, or building a stack of three or four thin sponges with different fillings, or making lemon drizzle using lots of lemon juice. A more surprising variant, the Poison Cake, has always been a favourite for small children's birthdays. Mum used to make it when we were little, and it was a funny, small drama when cut open to see a tasteless selection of colours in strong doses, for example blue, red and green. With a violently-coloured butter cream filling, say orange, and a vibrant icing coloured deep purple, this was perfect for a Halloween party!

I am currently tussling with the biggest bedspread so far, for Michael, the truth being that I am working so slowly that in the time since I started making quilts, my children are nearly grown-up. His is to be two-sided and both patchwork pieces are finished, needing only to be bound together. The first side has a swashbuckling quote from a soldier's memorial – 'They that do know their God shall be bold and do exploits' – sewn onto a collage of school shirts, old gym bags, first bathers, pyjama scraps and so on. The second side has 'Walk like Elvis' written across an Andy Warhol print, and Michael's name. Now that Michael's is nearly finished, I find I'm starting to think of what I might make for Kitty and Elizabeth; the planning and the collecting of the different pieces being a hugely enjoyable part of the whole project. I have managed to hang onto quite a few dresses from their childhoods, as well as tablecloths, shirts and other prints that they will probably remember, and I find that to me this feels like an important part of being their mother. Matthew has always kept photograph albums. They are lovely, and he is clear that in his photograph books it is always a sunny day. He has kept a record of all of our life together, with especial flair for the everyday, including work – meetings and all, oblivious to the march of digital technology, or rather, bending it variously to his purposes; he is always bang up-to-date and last weekend is often already printed out, edited and stuck in by Friday night.

It turns out that the quilts are my version of keeping the flame.

* * *

NO MORE DIRECTORS' DINING
ROOMS IN THE POTTERIES

D ID I NOTICE the industrial landscape before I
went to Stoke-on-Trent? I feel that I must have,
and I know that while biking around London as a student
I fell in love with all the stations, most especially St
Pancras, which I yearned for ardently. I badly wanted to
live in it, like a medieval princess with a time travel pass,
and I could not bear the idea that it was to be demolished. In about 1970 my brother Tom and I were taken
to the Roundhouse in Camden to see an all-male production of *As You Like It* (entirely in black and white, I think),
and when I heard subsequently that the building was to
be pulled down, I felt miserable. (Luckily it was
reprieved.)

I don't think I was particularly tuned in to the inheritance of the Industrial Revolution, but simply to the imperilled state of such places – in the same way that I felt so smitten with agony to think of the unloved and neglected state of, say, Melton Constable in Norfolk, where Desmond and I scrambled over the wall late one summer evening, startling the deer grazing under the broken windows of the big grand downstairs rooms where wallpaper hung in swathes. Any neglected farmyard filled me with longing, and stable yards with grass growing between the bricks and old saddles being nested in by mice induced a painful melancholy.

What captured my imagination about an abandoned and doomed building then (and now) was precisely the fact that it was still salvageable. But factories, mills and foundries, plus canals and all their appurtenances – I hadn't really thought about them until I went to Stoke for the first time to meet Sam.

Stoke-on-Trent railway station and the station hotel (which stands across the road) are a splendid pair of proud Victorian boasting buildings, successfully conceived to raise the spirits on arrival in the city. Or so it used to be. My mother-in-law worked as a designer for several of the potteries in the 1950s and early 1960s, bringing stylish sensibility to Spode and others, and she said that she particularly loved it when the train drew up there in a whoosh of steam. Her very first visit was to Minton, and in honour of the occasion Pat says she would have been wearing a clean pair of white gloves, which must have looked very snappy with her new suit from the department of Fortnum & Mason called Jeune Fille (Black Watch tartan with navy collar and cuffs). Her day would have included a delicious lunch on a proper tablecloth in the restaurant of the Potters Federation. In fact she can remember exactly what she ate: it was an *omelette aux fines herbes*. She remembered in startling detail the dining rooms of the grand potteries, and each of the meals she ate in them, saying how cosy it was to be offered a glass of sweet sherry to sip before lunch while the men warmed their bottoms in front of a coal fire. My lunch on my first visit would be an altogether more paltry affair – a Wrights meat and potato pie on Formica in the forlorn station café, if I was lucky. And as for my outfit, I cannot remember, but it was inadequate as I definitely felt cold – the weather was noticeably sharper than London. And the station had lowered its standards since Pat's day. It was predictably splattered with a thousand ugly notices, and the dignified and impressive war memorial – which incorporates an arch spanning the entrance with large brass plaques on either side to remember the Glorious Dead – was rudely ignored and could certainly have done with a major polishing session.

✳

My taxi took me to Chemical Lane (Sam's entirely evocative address) and on the way I craned my neck, trying to take in the view on both sides; I didn't want to miss anything. Until that day I had not seen urban squalor of this extent. Like a lot of people who live in the south of England, I had no idea what post-industrial Britain looked like. My idea of a city had at that time been formed in Oxford, Norwich, Bath, York and so on, and I was both shocked and fascinated. There were still lots of tall and chubby bottle-shaped kilns – the emblem of the Potteries – often in companionable clusters, many sprouting elders and buddleias but still standing. There were rows and rows of down-at-heel terraced houses, battered pubs, sad chapels converted into exhaust workshops, boarded-up churches and schools with chained-up gates and broken windows. The city sprawled along a spanking new dual carriageway and seemed to have no middle and blurry edges.

Since then the cosy bottle kilns have almost all gone, in the great demolition festival that has been bashing away at Stoke since the 1970s. The foundry at Longbridge was still firing in 1984, and the collieries at Wolstanton and Silverdale were still mining coal. But pottery, coal and steel were all declining rapidly by the time of my first visit, unemployment was rising and the whole place wore an air of grimy tumbledown neglect that seemed to me to be a vision of Cold War Eastern Europe. Meanwhile in London yuppies roared about in convertible cars and bankers racked up their bonuses in six-figure sums – how could this be the same country?

✳

On my way to Euston later in the afternoon I looked out of the train window much more beadily and realised that what Mrs Clark had said in geography lessons was true: the canal lay obediently beside the railway which had rendered it redundant within a mere 50 years of its heyday. The two transport options followed the valleys together, and it was obvious that the railway would have elbowed the canal aside because the canals looked so quaint and pixie-scale by comparison. I really wanted to walk along those towpaths and find out how to open a lock and operate a swing bridge. Before I managed that, I was to discover that there were still wharves and warehouses as well as factories standing along the Caldon and the Trent and Mersey canals which flow murkily through Stoke, and which were such a huge factor in the growth of the city during the nineteenth-century industrialisation of the local craft potteries. In Burgess and Leigh (where I bought plates for a while, because Sam was unwilling to make flatware), the warehouse beside the canal had piles of stencils – used for marking the packing cases with the destination countries – stacked up in the dirty windows. The warehousemen I spoke to there in the mid 1980s actually remembered straw-wrapping the pottery in wooden packing cases before loading them from the wharf onto narrow boats, even into the early 1950s. So the freight trade on the canals died a very long, slow death, and it felt as if the indignity and sadness of this decline was trampled into the towpaths.

A few years later, having dropped my car at a garage one morning on my way to work, I walked the last mile to our factory along the canal and thought about this sadness. The morning was bright, the hour was surely too early for rapists, but I slightly wished I had told someone where I was, and pushed to the back of my mind the strong admonishments of the mums in Oxford never to walk along the towpaths as they were lawless, nasty places. The path was overgrown in places, with old man's beard and brambles. I stopped to pick a handful of blackberries. There was a whiff of fox in the air, the dew winked on cobwebs busy with spiders and small birds scuffled in the elder bushes; there was no sign of a human and the traffic noise of the road died away behind me as I walked. This was a peaceful place, almost beautiful. The grassy path meandered on, past roofless buildings out of which great clouds of pigeons burst as I passed. I peered through the chain-link fence and was startled to see into a changing room where white coats still hung in rows, as if the shift was just about to come on; but the coats were crusted with bird poo and through the internal doorway I could see that most of the factory had been demolished. The towpath was a green corridor through a city which had forgotten that the canal was even there. When it was built, the canals were as important as the roads in terms of the activities of many of the city's businesses, with wharves accessing them at frequent intervals; but now it was fenced off and the buildings turned their backs, and fell to the demolition men.

So the packhorse loads were unstrapped and piled into the narrow boats, and then the railways jostled the canals into the background. But pretty quickly the roads came to dominate, so packing cases gave way to plastic trays in which the wares were transported down the motorways from the Midlands to the rest of the country. And then, within a startlingly short space of time, the traffic stopped; there was a pause as the containers mustered in the South China seas and we built new ports in Felixstowe and Southampton. Then the tide reversed and containers filled with foreign-made goods flooded in. And Stoke-on-Trent, like so many other Midlands cities, did not seem to have been alerted to the change of plan in time to get ready.

That was the sadness that hung like a mist along the canal. The whole city was almost as lost from view as a princess's castle in a fairy story, all hidden in tangled woods. To the buyers from the department stores all over the world, and to brides making their wedding lists, Staffordshire-made dinner services slid from sight.

During the pause, while world trade swung east, time had stopped in the Potteries; the casters and fettlers, along with the saggar maker's bottom-knockers, had all gone to sleep one day when the shift ended, and never woken up; they were never issued with their time travel passes. The city, which had been so important, had dropped from view, and the story of Britain seemed to have gone on without it.

Of course there never was a smoky meeting round a table where faceless bureaucrats ran a pencil through the mines and mills and factories of the Midlands and said, *The future is elsewhere, so this lot can sink or swim.*

But walking along the towpath beside the Caldon canal that early autumn morning, I felt as if that was what had happened and I felt a passionate desire to assert ever more proudly that we can and still should make pottery in Staffordshire.

The reversal from confident prosperity to widespread redundancy had happened amazingly quickly. Of course not all the potteries failed: some continued to prosper. The challenge is to do what the hotelware manufacturers have so triumphantly done, without faltering, which is to make a fantastic product and offer a great service so that the customers keep coming.

And certainly it's not all doom and gloom on the waterways. When Matthew and I walk on the canal north from Oxford, it is a purely idyllic experience, with king-fishers flitting between the willows, bank voles plopping in as you pass and plenty of come-hitherish waterside pubs. The locks are perfectly terrifying to operate, as there is such power in the rushing water, but the swing bridges are most satisfying and the engineering of every bridge and tunnel and handrail is poetic in its perfection. Indeed, when we hired a boat one half-term, we were told at the boatyard that there is now more traffic – albeit leisure, not freight – on the canals than when they were first opened.

PRINT, PATTERN AND LOTS

OF BRIGHT COLOURS

I'M GOING TO let rip about curtains for a moment. Bear with me because there is a helpful link to patterns on pottery. Here goes: Mum's kitchen at Bassingbourn in 1966 had lush curtains, made from generous lengths of navy blue mattress ticking. They fell in pleasing folds on the floor. The sofa under the window might have been covered in the same material; I can't remember. In Rawlinson Road she recycled some William Morris patterned curtains, which had belonged to Granny, and in the Minety kitchen, some blue-and-yellow-print bedroom curtains made a nice effortless reappearance. But those ticking curtains remained my ideal. I copied them myself on one of our moves, but didn't make them long enough, and they shrank when I washed them, which felt like jeans of the wrong length – just not cool. And the blinds I had made to go behind the sink strobed and flashed like a Bridget Riley painting, which was not relaxing. So it was time for a new idea when I next decorated a kitchen. Print, pattern, weaves, bright colours – ideally I want them all, and in no degree of moderation. And so the curtains in the kitchen of the barn conversion we did recently in Oxfordshire presented a good opportunity for a splurge.

I can't walk past Skandium on Marylebone High Street without going down into their basement to stroke the beautiful fabrics. I have, over the years, bought lengths of heavy cotton from there in many designs and used them with vast pleasure as tablecloths and curtains, or to drape over chairs and sofas. They are fiendishly expensive and completely delicious. The Swedish print company that I especially love is called Jobs Handtryck. It was founded in 1944, and it is now a third-generation family business devoted to high-quality furnishing fabrics. A three-metre length of the pattern called Pumpor, which is Pumpkins in Swedish, on a midnight-blue background has been one of my favourite tablecloths. I have Kastanj (Chestnut) on a white background pinned in a tall Gothic window, where it looks as if it has always been. So, with a feeling of thrilling abandon, I decided that our new kitchen curtains would be made in the Jobs Handtryck print called Rabarber

(Rhubarb) on a white background, lined with a pink ticking stripe to recall Bassingbourn a little. Each time I open or close the curtains, even secretly each time I walk through the room, the happy, bright, colourful confidence of this material makes my heart sing and dance.

This is the thing: my immoderate love of pattern spreads across all surfaces, and the richer the mix, the more inspired I feel. When planning a design to go on a mug, Matthew and I will draw our inspiration from all and every decorative tradition as we come across something exciting. I think that I was aware of and excited by patterns on fabrics, particularly printed cottons, long before I thought about decorating pottery, so textiles are a primary source of inspiration for me. And the story of textiles, especially that of block printing in the twentieth century, is such a rich vein; there is, I realised, a strong affinity between the technique of block printing on cotton and sponge printing on pottery. A block of wood, carved into a motif then flocked so that it will hold ink, creates a very similar rich and slightly fuzzy image to that created by repeating a cut sponge pattern on soft-fired earthenware.

The lineage of the twentieth-century textile designs that I like starts, of course, with William Morris, and from then on there is a recurrent mild theme of therapy, and creative living, which I find interesting. The artist Raoul Dufy is most thrilling, I think, when he bends his talents to designing textiles, and his work seems to me to be a recognisable beginning of the look of twentieth-century narrative textiles, with his Parisian scenes, and Shells and Sailors patterns.

In the dressing-up box in my childhood there was a very handwoven-looking pair of stout knickers and a tunic in a beautiful, deep orange linen, which Mum wore as a girl when she went to a dance class inspired by Isadora Duncan. I think Granny was always susceptible to artistic excitement, and I wish I knew more about what had been going on with those dancing lessons. But consequently I get a bit of a homey feeling from the pictures of the marvellously crazy, chiton-clad Raymond Duncan, Isadora's eccentric brother. I wish he had done more textile designs, but I love his wriggling figures on printed linen panels.

Of course, I have worshipped at the shrine of Bloomsbury and I particularly like the commercial project of the Omega Workshops. Then on to Phyllis Barron and Dorothy Larcher (oh, those Girton curtains!), who trained Enid Marx. My interest is shamefully shallow: I'm searching for flashes of personal revelation, sometimes by reference to names from my childhood, and these are some of the designers who have turned the lights on for me.

I flick on breathlessly through the swatches, then pause when I get to Nancy Nicholson, whose company Poulk Press was happily much more of a success than her previous venture, a grocery shop in Boars Hill outside Oxford. If it had not been, she and her children might have starved. She gives me a joyful feeling that well-loved household objects, such as a toy horse or a jug of flowers, make excellent subjects for designing. It helps that her father, the painter William Nicholson, was one of our chief household gods, and we often and often read his children's books *The Pirate Twins* and *Clever Bill*, both of which find strong echoes in his daughter's work. When I did the designs Knives and Forks, and Brown Kitchen, I was thinking along these lines.

Matthew and I have often stayed in Landmark Trust properties, especially relishing the occasional find of curtains handprinted by Lady Smith. It impresses me no end to think of her turning her hand to decorative textiles as an amateur, with such lovely results. Similarly, I very much admire the story of Jessie Brown, a gutsy nurse who started Yateley Textile Printers (now Yateley Industries) in the 1930s to create jobs for disabled workers, setting up a workshop for block printing cotton to make into household staples. When I visited this unusual set-up in the very early days of my company, with half a hope that they might want to decorate pottery for me in the workshops in Surrey, I was thrilled to realise that this was where lots of Mum's and Granny's nicest aprons, tablecloths and napkins came from.

My best textiles find ever was a pile of delicious teenage party dresses from the 1960s, some bearing the memorable label Dollyrockers, which just perfectly conjures up swinging London. These became instant dressing-up box favourites, veterans of plenty of parties, and they still sometimes feature in Emma Bridgewater catalogue shoots. I didn't know anything about the label – just loved the dresses – but Matt's mother shrieked with excitement when she saw them, as it turned out that she had worked for Sam Sherman, who owned the label, and she had designed lots of different patterns for the label. Sadly I didn't find a dress made in one of Pat's designs, but I think that my daughters Elizabeth, Kitty and Margaret give Sam Sherman's house model Patty Boyd a run for her money when they wear them!

The bold, bright patterns of these dresses filled me with delight and I longed to capture them in design. This was the starting point for Bright Flowers, Peace and Love, and Hearts and Flowers; all successful designs for us in 2005, 2006 and 2007. And I tell myself that I always actually need more decorative fabrics of all kinds, from tray cloths to bathing suits, as well as tablecloths, dresses and aprons; they are invaluable for styling catalogue pictures, so I have to keep shopping.

On an exciting family holiday driving across the Southern States, through the Carolinas, Louisiana, and southern Texas, Lizzy, Kitty and I fell on the vintage textiles and found treasures such as a sun bonnet made from pieces of old shirt cottons, countless lovely pinnies, old tea towels, and everywhere a richness of narrative prints featuring all sorts of unlikely motifs, from cowboys to kitchen utensils. A series of cowboy-inspired designs were an inevitability after this holiday.

And if you look closely, this very American style of narrative textile design has links straight back to Dufy. Along with many others, I hugely admire and love Cath Kidston's contemporary take on this type of narrative pattern, which she makes her own so successfully with her fetching colours.

I hope that the whole range of Emma Bridgewater designs is based on a good mood; a mood of welcome, informality and pleasurable hospitality. But each time I set about finding and making a new pattern, I have to be specific. The task is fascinating, encapsulating the challenge to be completely familiar and at the same time completely new. When I go to Venice, or Paris, or Austin, or any of the cities I choose to visit for inspiration – whether alone, with Matthew or as a family – I am always alert and on the lookout for clues which might seed a new idea, but I am unlikely to theme a product or pattern as Parisian, Venetian, Texan or anything as linked as that. Instead, those vibrant experiences charge me up with a deeper desire to find a true expression of where I come from. That is a constant; the intensity ebbs and flows, but the designs are the outward face of a long-term longing to tell you what I like currently, and how I feel.

The first patterns I made were based on repeats and combinations from the following, distinctly odd, group of motifs: a bow with trailing ribbons; a patterned diamond; a simple triangle; a prawn; a running gypsy dog; and some other animals such as a rabbit, a fox and a monkey. At first I simply clung to the rim of each piece, building up border patterns of varying simplicity, echoing the cosy look of old spongeware. But then one day I broke away, let go of the edge and struck out, when I saw the freedom afforded by a set of printing blocks and a selection of underglaze ceramic colours in a traditional palette. I developed a range of colours inspired by traditional spongeware pottery: cobalt blue, deep sea green, brown, grey, golden yellow and (always hardest) a deep red – not rosy enough, in fact leaning towards maroon, but it is chemically the biggest challenge to make a good red.

As I swiftly mastered my new-found technique, my designs developed. My first breakthrough was Chintz, a faded-looking rose with a ragged leaf, which I used to conjure an atmosphere of comfy sofas full of dogs sleeping in front of a fire. When I called it Chintz, I was half-conscious of imitating the free feeling of a piece of printed furnishing cotton. The fruit design of Figs, and Vine which followed, was channelling William Morris, whilst thinking about the relaxed feeling of my favourite gardens, at the best moment of the end of the summer. Then Farmyard and Hunting, with bands of animals chasing each other around; the idea sprang from my love of Randolph Caldecott's lively illustrations for children's books such as *John Gilpin*. Some themes are universal – actually most are; the thrill is in finding a personal interpretation. My technique opened up the whole panoply of flowers with a new look built in: once I'd seen the way that I could scatter my sponge prints so freely in Chintz, I went straight for my favourite flowers, namely Morning Glory, Lilies and Tulips. More recently I was moved to do patterns of Zinnias and Sweet Peas by Matt's outrageously gorgeous gardening.

Matthew's mother came to visit my studio in early 1986, which was before I met him. She came because at that time I was talking to the National Trust about some designs, and as their designer-in-chief she wanted to check me out. She was kind, encouraging and funny, and she looked exactly as her designs had let me to expect her to – cosy, stylish, domesticated and keen on cats. In passing she remarked that I had definitely scored a first by using a potato as a decorative motif in the design called Scattered Veg. I did one design with chickens before I met Matthew – it's called Black Cockerel – but since then I've left the poultry to him.

It was around the time that I turned 40 that I remembered the feeling of Ladybird Books with some kind of rather fierce nostalgia. The outcome of sinking myself all over again into *Shopping with Mother* and *The Party* (whose pictures brought back sharp and clear the thrill of realising that I could read) in 2003 was a pattern called Circus, as well as the Anemone and Fireworks designs. However, my affectionate feelings about 1960s suburbia had already been expressed in Polka Dots, which came out in 2002.

Thinking about the kitchen curtains again, I wonder if I could do something with rhubarb?

STALKING FIGS

THE SUMMER that I was 16, Desmond had the roofers in. The highest platform of the scaffolding made an excellent new place to have tea or drinks; so when the men departed at the end of the day, Desmond intrepidly led us up the ladders and then hauled the provisions up after us in a basket. His other house is seventeenth-century, with elegant gables, and awfully tall. It makes my heart skip a beat to think of it now – all those steep ladders and such a long way to the top, but the view from up there was an incomparable thrill. We could see out to sea across the marshes, up to Blakeney, down to Cley and all around the farm. We could see Reggie going home and Chloe picking up fallen peaches;

and as we scanned the garden all around the house, it seemed much more likely that this was just the present version of the house and its gardens in this extraordinary, wonderful place.

Desmond had shown me the doorways and walls which predate the house and hint at some earlier incarnation, and I had found it hard to make any real sense of this – just as in childhood I had essentially disbelieved the legend that the little village of Cley, next along the coast from Wiveton, was once a nationally significant port, with big ships plying important trade along the Baltic coast. Neither fact seemed likely, and I could not summon up any kind of picture of the past in either place. But I could believe in there having been boats on the harbour at the mouth of the River Glaven once Mum had pointed out to us the choirboys' graffiti on a panel in Salthouse church showing crude but lively representations of two-and three-masted sailing ships. Similarly from the roof of Desmond's house we could see that the present garden overlaid earlier plans. The lovely old brick path running diagonally across the kitchen garden and coming to a quiet halt at a peartree in the corner probably predated the garden itself, and might have been going purposefully towards a distant and long-gone destination; maybe the Carmelite Friary of Blakeney, whose ruins were beneath the campsite next door and in approximately the right direction.

Rick always said that waking up at Wiveton gave him

a special feeling of ancient peace. I tried to analyse this feeling, thinking perhaps it had as much to do with the atmosphere created by the sound of the pigeons, endlessly amorous in the tall trees on two sides of the house, or the evocative calls of oystercatchers, curlews and other marsh birds among the cattle out beyond the garden. But somehow the view from the roof explained that the past really is a part of the place, and when you went out to pick a lettuce, you were walking in ancient, maybe monkish-sandalled, footsteps. All around the house and its fields and gardens you waded through layers of time. Perhaps this was the key to the extraordinary feeling of something complete and set apart that envelops the place, making it the perfect house in which to dream away teenage summers.

We spent at least a fortnight there every year, in August usually, and it set standards of happiness and loveliness that I thought at the time were just normal life, not realising that here was a place that I would never improve on, that was in fact setting an image of domestic perfection that I would chase after forever.

There were perfect, deep windowsills in which to hide behind the curtains to discover the sexy bits in DH Lawrence, Nabokov, Henry Green and JP Donleavy. I loved the novels on yellow paper gathering dust by the bedsides, and the piles of faded fashion magazines, and even the fishing and shooting books in distant loos behind green baize doors. I was hungry for fiction, and searched the second-hand bookshops in Holt, Fakenham and Burnham Market for out-of-print lady novelists, historical bodice-rippers. I read all of Thomas Hardy, then switched happily to HE Bates. My preferred window seat looked down into a sunken garden which was sheltered, full of cistus, phlox, lavender and roses, and bathed in sun at tea time.

Desmond taught me to drive in his Ford Consul around the farm. We went out at night in the same car, bouncing out onto the marshes at Morston, with Kris Kristofferson singing 'Me and Bobby McGee' on a cassette, to meet friends coming home from a day's sailing with a bucket of mackerel to cook on a fire. The evening would be spent laughing and joking, passing around a bottle of Bell's and smoking Player's No 6 cigarettes.

There were always duties to do in the kitchen garden (in between reading orgies and picnics and swimming expeditions) – peas to pick and shell, broad beans to pod, redcurrants to string, strawberries and peaches to lay carefully in a trug. I simply loved to trail around behind Chloe carrying baskets and colanders. Just as I loved to watch her cooking. She makes the very best jam and jelly you have ever tasted, somehow through care and attention persuading them to set with the minimum of sugar, preserving the deliciousness of mulberries, damsons, raspberries and the rest without smothering them in sugar.

There have been lots of nice changes to the inside of the house over the years, but during those early summer holidays, all of the domestic arrangements were simple to the point of austerity. Mum and I took the washing to Holt to do in the launderette. Once when we arrived, Chloe took Mum to see some 'great improvements' that had been made to the laundry arrangements, and with a flourish opened one of the back doors to reveal – a new washing line.

The stove, in a dark corner of the kitchen, needed coaxing to get one or two of the rings to work, the grill had been abandoned and all in all it was a precarious business to cook for the sometimes considerable numbers. Yet, as Mum observed, Chloe could weave a spell over the carcass of a bantam, some shot lettuces, a handful of herbs, an egg and half a lemon to produce the most delicious, bright green lettuce soup finished with avgolemono to a very slightly thickened consistency. Then, to complete the sorcery, she served the soup in thin, pale, French porcelain two-handled cups on saucers – every meal was an essay in restraint and elegance.

Long before this delicious fruit and veg cornucopia started to become as it is now – almost standard in expensive supermarkets – Chloe and Desmond were living an austere and particular version of la dolce vita at Wiveton. Dorothy Hartley's meticulous and beautifully illustrated book *Food in England* reminds us that lightly boiled asparagus, artichokes with melted butter, quince cheese, elderflower cordial, endive salad, mulberry jelly, whitecurrants, raspberries, damsons, and a thousand other delicacies, were in truth a part of our culinary heritage that had always existed behind the high walls of private gardens.

Without referring to the subject, by the end of August pretty much everyone would be paying their own solitary, watchful daily visits to the special places – in the yard, along a lane and inside the kitchen garden – where at last the figs were coming to perfection of ripeness. Visible and tantalising from early July, the figs have to be almost overripe to hit the peak of deliciousness, by which time all the birds, not to mention the other human watchers, know all about it, as do the wasps – so the race is on. This was and is the quintessence of Wiveton, picking warm, bursting figs from among the shadowy leaves, knocking the wasps out and biting into that sweet bruise.

I have said that my pottery designs are an evocation of my mother's kitchen and her hospitable warmth, and it's completely true, but at the same time I have also had Wiveton, Desmond and Chloe in mind. The Figs design, conceived when I was breaking out of the constriction of early repeating spongeware patterns, discovering the joyful, simple freedom that hand printing offered, was an expression of all those blissful teenage summers.

Desmond has recently transformed a big barn, built by his parents in the 1950s when they bought their first combine; these days it is a colourful and welcoming café where you can have a delicious meal, with many of the ingredients just picked from the surrounding fields. There is a shop where you can buy all sorts of treats, including the best jam, and plants which might have been grown in the kitchen garden across the yard. You can find it on the coast road between Blakeney and Cley; look out for the signs 'Wiveton Farm Shop and Café' – it is perfection.

VOTES FOR WOMEN

CINNAMON (with top notes of vanilla and carpet-cleaning chemicals) is the smell of American trade fairs. Emma Bridgewater showed at the New York Gift Show twice a year for several years during the 1990s. It was dispiriting, as we were usually tucked away amongst a rather defensive British section, in a slightly out-of-the-way place deep in the Javitts Center, with few visitors and very few customers. My consolation, especially when manning the stand alone for a week, was a trio of diners where I could stop to have a tip-top American breakfast on my walk from the Red Roof Inn to the exhibition centre, so when my alarm went, I sprang out of bed at the thought of hickory-smoked bacon strips with pancakes and maple syrup. After this I could happily spend the rest of my day immersed in a book (which might have been Isabel Allende, whose strange magical world was potent enough at that time to keep the other stall holders at arm's length). Of course what I was really warding off were thoughts of home, and the paralysingly awful guilt which inevitably twines with the image of my children going to bed without me there to read them a story, having breakfast cooked by someone else, going to school and I'm not driving them. . . I learned that I shared these pangs with every single other mother whose work takes her away from home, but never how to avoid them.

On one of these trips I met an inspiring woman called Mrs Mottahedeh. She had a huge personal collection of beautiful china, and her business focused on reproducing some of these old designs to very high standards. Although this is not my cup of tea exactly, she was enthusiastic about the incredible craftsmanship available in the Far East, and I am interested to think of this going on at the same time as the rush amongst so many British manu-facturers to have things made ever more cheaply in the same places. I preferred her project to theirs. And more-over she gave me a plate that I especially loved. It was a facsimile of a plate designed by Emmeline Pankhurst's daughter Christabel, for sale to help raise funds for the

Suffragette Movement. It bears the simple slogan 'Votes for Women' in a restrained Edwardian script. I took this home and discussed its appeal with Matthew. How, we wondered, did we come up with a phrase or slogan with the right resonance for 1994? The eventual result, after several versions, was the first five pieces in the Toast & Marmalade range. The very first piece was the side plate, which describes our completely favourite breakfast, in two versions. Toast and Marmalade is simple, a combination of which you can never tire, whilst Kedgeree is also delicious and very English, with its faint memory of the Raj, as well as being a most satisfactory combination of letters.

When I jumped back in to run the company myself again just after Michael was born, one of the first things I did was to look at the margins on export sales and, with pleasure, decide that they were far too low. This made it easy to cancel all overseas sales activity, which spared me another trip to the Javitts Center. But it was still impossible to manage the factory and the commercial office without spending an awful lot of time away from home.

HAVING IT ALL?

By a very long mile, the question most often put to me, usually by other working women, is,

How on earth do you manage to balance the demands of

185

work with the exhausting commitment of a family?

And I never know the answer. There isn't one. During the past 50 years, women in large numbers have taken on unprecedented workloads whilst upping the ante in every other conceivable area of life, from home-making, gardening and cooking to keeping up with the book club, looking a million dollars and enjoying a riotous sex life with absolutely no quarter given at any stage, or a sign on the horizon that we might ever slack off. I feel pretty sure that this is unsustainable, and self-inflicted, even though it feels as if the pressures come from outside us.

When I feel maddest with exhaustion, I think of Mum, who was a champion at getting up early, exercising several horses, baking the bread, making a stew for supper and then mowing the lawns; and I remind myself that she would definitely have taken to the sofa for a nice rest after lunch. Or in front of the telly as soon as the racing started. Or after supper. Or even halfway through supper – she would fall asleep on the kitchen sofa and snore more and more loudly until we woke her and evicted her, at which point she would be rather grumpy about being disturbed. And I know perfectly well that I need to be on that sofa. . .

All I can offer are some of the ideas for guilt and exhaustion mitigation that I have evolved over the years. And most of them are hardly what I could call All My Own Work.

A JOINT ENTERPRISE

Firstly, and painfully for some, as this is not a very popular item with the sisterhood, my career has worked because I married a man who really truly wants me to have a successful career. The reality has often been surprisingly tough, but it has been survivable only because this was always in place. So, choose very carefully, girls!

Despite Votes for Women, and the whole panoply of anti-discrimination legislation, women are (as we all discuss exhaustively) still not at all clear about how we can ever manage to play an equal role with men. In the unhappy phases when Matt and I were both struggling at separate projects, scrabbling with each other for a bigger share of the scant time available away from home and raising the children, it was impossible. Somehow we arrived at the realisation that we can only make it all work if we regard our whole life – including home, the children and both of our careers – as a Joint Project. We have taken this to both extremes: having worked closely together initially, followed by nine years when I ran the company while he spent more time at home, we then swapped and Matt has been in charge since 2008.

So there is everything to be said for talking it through. Again and again. Long car journeys, at night preferably, are profitable. Or walk and talk. We have always found it possible to progress our ideas best if we are also in motion.

BUY MORE SOFAS

Secondly, what you really, really need is somewhere to sit down, for heaven's sake. You think I'm banging on too much about that sofa, but I'm serious. Matthew doesn't really see any point in sitting down except to eat, immediately before passing out for a solid night's sleep. It dawned on me after several years of marriage that I violently disagree with him on this. On holiday in the Southern States of the USA we all developed serious porch envy. In talking about this, and what we found so appealing about the porches of all descriptions on every house we saw, we realised that we desperately wanted and needed to hang out, lounge around, do nothing in particular – which is what a stoop is for.

So when we got home we put a large veranda on the south side of the house. Never mind that Matthew had simultaneously seen it as a great place to have enormous parties, we dragged two big sofas out there in April and they stayed out until October. And it worked for all of us; it became the nicest place to be, and there being no sink to hand, there is no washing-up in sight. We sat around and chatted as never before. And it doesn't need to stop at the veranda; you can be aware of making places to sit and talk all around the house and garden. Window seats in particular are very appealing places to sit and chat, or read, or sip a cup of tea.

HURRAY FOR GRANDPARENTS

Thirdly, you will always be happier if the someone else looking after your kids while you work is a member of your family. When we stopped renting in Worstead, decided to put down roots in Norfolk and bought the house in the nearby village of Wickmere (ironically only a year before I realised it was time for me to shoulder the respon- sibility of managing the company again), Matthew's parents followed suit and moved to the next-door village. I was at first startled, as this was not a move we had talked about, and frankly it seemed that my mother-in- law would be a little close for comfort. . . I could not have been more wrong.

Pat could see, better than I, just how tough this was, for the children especially, and as a working mum herself she wanted to help. She and Peter made their house a cosy haven for our children, and the younger two had a bedroom of their own there, with pyjamas and dressing gowns hanging behind the door and toothbrushes in the bathroom. Together Pat and Peter did far more school runs than Matt or I did, went to many more concerts and sports days, and always had an enticing and impres- sive creative project on the go with the children for good measure. As a result they have their own unmediated relationships with all four children. I think that this is more unusual than it might be, as we are some of us growing away from the mechanics of the extended family and we can be awkward about offering and accepting help – at least, I know that I was. But Pat and Peter bust through my foolishness and made all the difference. And it seems that while the guilt you feel when working away from home and family is unavoidable (it would be a bit bleak if both parents could skip away lightheartedly, I guess), it is lessened immensely if the children are in such idyllic circumstances as mine often were, thanks to Matt's amazing parents.

MUM, THERE'S NO WEETABIX LEFT

Fourthly, I suggest that you should drop your domestic standards. What can I say? The fact is that my house is often a tip. It's horribly hard, I have found, to stop judging yourself by the muddle in the airing cupboard, the unironed napkins and pillowcases, the fluff under the beds, the moths munching away in every drawer and cupboard, the curtains which you have not yet got around to finding or making, and all the rest of it. But for me it seems helpful to admit defeat sometimes, and to desist from trying to keep up an image of perfect domesticity. I have learned to like normality, with all its piles of dry-cleaning still to be dropped off, unmatched socks, malfunctioning dishwasher and stains on the carpets. I focus on the things I like doing, such as making bread, sewing on name tapes while cuddled up in front of the telly, making vanilla sugar and ensuring that there is almost always some really delicious tea and a packet of digestives in the kitchen.

IT'S OUT OF YOUR HANDS

Fifthly, you have to let whoever takes the helm while you work do it their way, especially if it is your beloved – don't even think about trying to exert long-distance controls.

I sympathise with the friends who wail that the children watch too much TV and eat supper far too late at night while their father is in charge (and of course he hasn't done the washing-up, or washed their uniforms either) and I often join in. But somehow we have to let go. This came home forcibly when I rang Matt's mobile one October morning to talk to them all as they drove to school, only to find that they were cooking sausages on a fire on the beach a mile from school, and yes, they did all have wet socks, and not a coat between them. Someone else (another mum, for certain) provided dry socks, and they were all having a really blissful time. One of the hardest things is smiling through the jokes about the beloved au pair being the children's real mum, or dad – we have had some amazing au pair boys – because I learned that I had to let my children love other people as much as they love me.

A DECENT ALIBI

If, like me, you don't have any hobbies, it's time you invented some, even making patchwork quilts. . . We will call that Tip Number Six. A hobby is merely an alibi, as all fishermen know, a cover story for sloping off and pleasing yourself for a while. This can get lost in the hurly-burly of work and family, and you may have to think cleverly to find the occupation that supplies some of the missing personal satisfaction that I'm talking about here. I like to have a physical, tangible result to show for my time out, hence patchwork.

DON'T TAKE OUT MEMBERSHIP AT A GYM

For me a gym is the third circle of hell, and provides endless internal excuses for not quite getting around to taking exercise. But exercise you must! Roughly speaking you need to feel normal again by the end of every day, and don't let the pressure build up. A swim, a run or, really best of all, a walk is a good way to shake off the stress which accumulates during the day. If you don't look after yourself, very simply and definitely, you will get ill. I did not believe this, pushed on through the usual stress symptoms of escalating dizzy spells, increasing unease and sleeplessness, unhappiness and moodiness. I had been brought up to think of myself as needing less maintenance than the car, or the dishwasher, with all ills cured by an early night. But even an early night seemed like a luxury I did not have time for. So I hammered on without heeding the distress signals until my immune system suffered, after which I developed a mild form of rheumatoid arthritis, which I still ignored, and soon I found I was pretty much immobilised. In fact, as one of my sisters trained for the London Marathon, I realised that I could scarcely walk, let alone run. It was bliss to hand over the running of the business to Matthew and rediscover myself through a period in which I concentrated on how to feel better. The drugs to control rheumatoid arthritis are demanding, but in my case very effective. Suffice it to say that I now exercise regularly, even including running, and I feel fantastic.

Anyway, take heed if you are experiencing weird symptoms. This is stress.

FRIDAY NIGHT SUPPER

I can't possibly express this as an anti-stress tip – it's much too vital and central – but it is part of the story of building a company whilst raising a family, and of surviving that roller-coaster ride. When I started up, I imagined that the business would politely step back when I needed to spend time at home. Other people ran the company and enabled this for the first 12 years, but at a certain point I had to commit personally to growing the company. And after that the pressure on me grew steadily, making the split between work and home tougher to manage.

Whatever the work demands, I now know that I want to put the family first more often. Make more time. Have more meals together. Eat meatballs. And lentils!

On the Friday nights when I find myself listening to Jonathan Dimbleby orchestrating *Any Questions?* on BBC Radio Four from a church hall in a far-flung market town, while I make the two sauces for this recipe, knowing that in cars and trains from different places some or all of my family are heading home for the weekend, I feel very happy. Since Kitty and Margy gave up eating meat more than two years ago, I have made lentils-like-mince separately alongside the meatballs and using similar herbs, as lentils too are good with the tomato sauce.

MEATBALLS WITH TWO SAUCES
SERVES 6–8

* * *

FOR THE MEATBALLS

Put 450g beef mince (not too lean) and 450g lamb mince into a large bowl and mix roughly with a wooden spoon. Add a medium egg (beaten), a slosh of olive oil (1 tablespoon), 2 crushed garlic cloves, some finely chopped green herbs (e.g. rosemary, sage and coriander), plus ½ teaspoon of chilli flakes if you like, and some salt and pepper. Stir together and cover while you make the tomato sauce.

FOR THE TOMATO SAUCE

Heat a slosh of olive oil (2 tablespoons) in a heavy saucepan. Add a finely chopped onion and sweat it down slowly in the oil over a low heat for 10 minutes, stirring occasionally. Pour in 2 tins chopped tomatoes and stir. Sprinkle in 1 teaspoon of brown sugar, a squirt of tomato purée (about 1 tablespoon), salt and pepper and some chopped fresh oregano. Simmer for about 40 minutes, or longer if possible, adding a little olive oil occasionally.

Form the seasoned mince into walnut-sized balls, roll them lightly in flour and arrange tightly in a deep-sided baking tray or small roasting tin with a little oil in it, while it heats gently over a flame. Put the full tray into a medium-hot oven set at 190°C/170°C fan/gas 5 for 20 minutes, or until the meatballs are browned. Remove and pour off any excess fat, but do not move the balls or scrape the pan! Set aside. Check the tomato sauce, stir and add a little more olive oil.

FOR THE CHEESE SAUCE

Melt 100g butter in a pan, stir in 85g plain flour and cook gently for half a minute. Gradually stir in 800–850ml of milk. Add a sprig of fresh bay leaves (about 6 leaves), bring to the boil, stirring all the time, and leave to simmer gently for 5 minutes. Stir in 175g grated Cheddar, 1 tablespoon of English mustard and some salt and pepper.

Assemble the dish by pouring the tomato sauce over the meatballs, then the cheese sauce over the top, and grating a generous amount of cheese – about 75g – on top of that (I like to use Parmesan). Bake in a medium-hot oven set at 200°C/180°C/ gas 6 for about 30 minutes or until browning, crispy and delicious. Serve with plain rice.

LENTILS-LIKE-MINCE
SERVES 2 AS A MAIN COURSE,
OR 3–4 AS A SIDE DISH

* * *

Heat 3 tablespoons of olive oil in a medium-sized pan over a medium heat. Add 1 bunch of trimmed and thinly sliced skinny spring onions (or 3 larger salad onions) and 2 cloves of thinly sliced garlic and cook gently for 2–3 minutes until the garlic just starts to colour. Now stir in a generous handful of chopped green herbs (rosemary, sage, coriander). Add 225g Puy lentils and stir them around, to coat them in oil, then add 600ml cold water. Bring to the boil, lower the heat and simmer gently for 30–35 minutes, stirring now and then, until the lentils are tender and all the water has been absorbed. Check that the water is not evaporating too quickly whilst the lentils are cooking, and add a tiny bit more if necessary. Once they're tender, stir in ½ teaspoon of salt, cover the pan, take off the heat and leave to sit for 5 minutes. Serve with a spoonful of the tomato sauce.

KELBURN GRANNY'S
CHINA SHOES

JUST 15 MINUTES before the Glasgow train was due to leave, I pulled into a parking space behind Euston, jumped out of the car, pumped some francs into the meter until the Out of Order sign clanked up red, scrawled a note saying 'Meter bust' to put in my windscreen, popped the cassette out of the machine, grabbed my suitcase and, after locking the door, legged it for the train. I arrived on the platform out of breath. I spotted a crowd of familiar covert coats and fur hats congregating further down the train. It was my aunts and uncles, and – thinking that I was about to spend two days with them – I dived hastily into the nearest carriage, chucked my case in the rack and sank down into the comforting sadness

and squalor of *Good Morning Midnight*. I love my Scottish cousins deeply, but I felt outnumbered and antisocial and not up to immersion just yet. Jean Rhys's company suited me better for the journey.

At Glasgow station I was overwhelmed by memories of waiting there for Granny and David (her third husband), with whom we spent several holidays in the care of an agency nanny we adored called Miss Hoskins. She was old-fashioned enough to make everyone secure in the illusion that the 1920s had never ended, as she adhered tightly to an *ancien régime* we had never had, of nursery walks, after-lunch rests, drawing room visits and matching kilts and Shetland jerseys for Sophy and me. In the car hire office I was given the key to a tiny car I could hardly afford, but knew I could not afford to be without, and a hopeless map which enabled me to get thoroughly lost before eventually finding my way out of the city along the derelict Clydebank towards the west coast.

Arriving at Kelburn I let myself into the hall and paused on my way towards the broad stairs leading up to the drawing room, where I knew everyone would be having tea. I put my head around the door of the gun room, and the battered rows of Barbours and boots all steeped in gun oil emitted a powerful genie who laughed, coughed, greeted me kindly and teasingly asked me in a gravelly voice if I could remember the names of the different deer and goats whose horns and antlers, pronged, twisted and hooked, hung all up the stairs amongst constellations of swords and knives. David had been a kind, steady figure, oblivious to the alarums and excursions of family life. He always treated me as if he liked my company, and I enjoyed the grown-up talks we had about the estate and its neighbours as we walked up the Glen, or around the garden inspecting the enormous trees. One Christmas Mum had suggested *The Rocky Horror Show* to Granny as an alternative to my customary trip with her and David to the ballet at Covent Garden, and as Tim Curry gyrated in suspenders just inches from our aisle-side seats, David feigned dropping his cigar lighter a couple of times to get out of the firing line of the pelvic thrusting, but remained smiling throughout. Now he was gone. I patted the head of the stuffed alligator and set off up the stairs. Outside the drawing room door I instinctively paused again and tapped the chronometer on the chest. Its little pointy finger jerked and scratched, but the ink had run dry and it left no mark to say whether the pressure was going up.

The family was gathered around the fire at the far end of the room, and I could see Granny in their midst like a tiny little old dolly folded up between two people on the faded brocade sofa, with her handbag at her side as ever. There was a rush of kindness –

Emma, darling, well done. Come and have a cup of tea.

Mum, look, Emma is here. She just arrived.

And surprise –

Where have you sprung from? A hire car, but why on earth? Is your father here too, or are you on your own?

Amidst explanations –

I want to be useful; maybe I can drive people or flowers or orders of service back and forth. So silly of me, useless map, lost in the Gorbals, you can imagine! No, Pop is away in Australia; impossible for him to get back.

I made my way to kiss Granny and accepted some tea in an elegant china teacup, so like her and so much of a piece with her collection of vases, not far away in the flower room, all nymphs and shepherds and rococo twiddling. Sniffing the delicious cigar smoke from Granny's unabated cigarillos and the wood smoke from the fire, I felt happy and familiar, but also slightly apart. I loved the house – the ghosts, the smell of it, even the feeling that my family were very short-term visitors in the long history of a lovely place – and realised as I perched on a stool in front of the fire at Granny's feet that my connection with it was ebbing and would soon be severed. She was so small suddenly. Whilst always spirited, she was obviously losing her once-firm grip, and when she died, David's son from his first marriage would gently eject his step-siblings and their children.

∗

Very early after supper Granny went to bed. She was sleeping now in the night nursery, just behind the dining room – where we had slept, with Miss Hoskins in the room next door – as she could no longer manage the stairs. It was strange to feel her life merging in old age with ours as children. I sat and held her hand, and we talked about the funeral flowers while my mind wandered, and I realised that she and David had been a happy and companionable couple.

As a student I often bicycled from my digs in Bloomsbury to have supper with them in Cheyne Walk, where the television news programmes and the stately dance of the drinks tray set the pattern for the evening. Their midday pink gin gave way to whisky at six, and I would have a small (pretty, ornately cut) glass of white wine, hock probably – flowery, not very dry. Supper, which was always timed to end before the BBC Nine O'Clock News, was insignificant in terms of food, in which neither Granny nor David seemed to have much interest. There might have been rissoles, or fish in a pale sauce, with maybe some frozen peas. The real nourishment, the whisky, continued uninterrupted, with more wine for me. I can only actually picture Granny eating a few shreds of smoked salmon, but I suppose she ate supper. After the news we might have some Charbonnel et Walker violet creams by way of pudding, then soon after that I would wobble off into the night, knowing that they were happily bickering about politics and David would be pouring the final drink of the evening.

Her house in London was, like her teacups and vases at Kelburn, a consistent reflection of her taste for feminine formality and lots of pretty decoration; the panelling was painted eau-de-Nil, the pictures were misty landscapes, the bathrooms smelt of Floris jasmine bath oil and the furniture was eighteenth-century, much covered with her collection of elaborately gilded and painted china shoes, and whole hiring fairs of shepherdesses. She had lots of pretty, formal china and never deviated from matching services – cups with their correct saucers, dessert plates, butter knives, the whole panoply of formal feeding equipment complete with silver pheasants marching down the table amongst the little formal posies of small flowers – and it seems of a piece that the food itself was unimportant. I guess any of us could struggle through perfectly happily on a diet of scrambled eggs and smoked salmon, or quail's eggs with Melba toast somewhere to hand. I knew I was committed to a different food culture, but loved dropping into their routine; it was a contented and a different life.

The funeral the next morning was austere: David was reclaimed by his naval career and his family. Granny bore witness to their dashing alliance in black astrakhan and lots of diamonds, but only the men went with his coffin to the burial ground. Of course I know that this is the Scottish custom, but it served to heighten my instinct that he was drawing back into Kelburn and we were lingering only a little while longer before being set aside. In a thin, cold drizzle I walked around the Plaisance – the walled garden – for the last time but it was too cold for even a wisp of the mysterious smell from the myrtle bushes, so I slipped out of the door nearest to the kitchen garden and hurried around the mournful, empty green-houses, past the beds where Granny used to have rows of gladioli for picking to arrange in her ornate vases around the house (along with the usual roses, lilies, asters, tulips and ferns). I knew that they were anathema to my other granny, but secretly I found their *Come Dancing* colours of salmon pink, pillar-box red, mauve and pale yellow quite delicious. I remembered spending a spring fortnight picking daffs at Kelburn, bunching them in twelves with little elastic bands, laying them in boxes and then driving to Ayr with Granny to sell them to a florist, and wondered why grannies are so strongly linked to flowers – and felt that this was as it should be. Then I went inside to hold Granny's hand again for a while before slipping away, back to the world of mugs.

Kelburn Granny died within the year and in her will she left me £10,000. This went straight into the business.

Through the tinkle of coffee spoons with ebony beans on them, in the saucers of pink and gold Sèvres china cups, I can hear her and David in a chuckling, throaty chorus of loving encouragement, little as they esteemed earthenware or informality.

*** * * ***

MY, BUT MISS MEAKIN,
YOU'RE BEAUTIFUL

I CAN'T REMEMBER Mum and Pop's first kitchen in Cambridge, or the next one in Chiswick. By coincidence this was just around the corner from the house in Hammersmith Terrace where Matt's parents lived. We must have passed each other in our prams, or fed the ducks alongside each other on Chiswick Mall. Then when I was about three, Mum and Pop moved to Hertfordshire and bought a pretty farmhouse in a village called Bassingbourn. Perhaps because Granny regarded the kitchen as daunting, Mum seems to have been very confident about hers. In fact I think it was at this precise time that Mum re-invented the whole idea of The Kitchen. With a bit of help from her friends, who are captured in my memory as impossibly glamorous – all backcombed hair, Gucci handbags, Mexicana ruffles and thick black eyeliner, wafting in delicious clouds of Joy, with Dusty Springfield on the gramophone. They all instinctively knew that the future was easygoing and informal, and that they would be in charge and having a ball in their own kitchens.

Mum kept the good features of the kitchen that had been left after the last farmer's wife had departed, such as the red and black flagged floor, the huge pitch pine dresser which was built in, and occupied a whole wall, and the draught screen which folded out to keep the farmer cosy by the fire in the next door dining room. The farmer's widow, Mrs Russell, only went as far away as a bungalow she had had built on the far side of some of the barns, where, along with her sister, she lived quietly and rather dimly behind thick net curtains. I loved going to visit them to drink orange squash and examine their little elephants made out of ivory – maybe her sister had come home from a different life, in a different bungalow, in India.

But very little else of the farm remained after Mum had painted the kitchen walls dark pink, the colour of her favourite pudding at the time: blackcurrant fool. And she put in fat, curvy white melamine surfaces and a new big white Aga, which ran on coke and necessitated an exciting dash through to the back door with a pan full of hot ash after riddling, twice every day. I remember the arrival of the Hotpoint clothes washing machine (better than all the ones that came after it, she said), which meant no more mangling the wet clothes when they came out of the twin tub; and there was a stable door, where the bantams often perched as we fed them on the paving stones outside. Her china was still a conventional dinner service, with some additional big, blue Danish coffee cups. However, she was already buying old china. She covered the built-in dresser with the remains of a service in a pretty Copeland-type pattern called Spot and Wreath, which – as well as plates and dishes – consisted of meat plates and dear little covered tureens on stands.

After Mum and Pop divorced, my brother Tom, sister Sophy and I lived with Mum in Oxford, and spent every third weekend, as well as half of the school holidays, at Pop's house in Bassingbourn. He married again; Lucy was glamorous, beautiful and strong-minded, and as she moved into the house with Pop, it was inevitable that she would make changes. It was surprising to find my bedroom completely transformed with bold, flowery wallpaper on all the uneven sloping walls and even on the ceiling, with the old furniture standing in the barn. But it was also good fun, as Lucy made a completely new and deeply fantastic dressing-up box and encouraged us to put on plays, and she made a Super 8 film of us fooling around in the garden. She also painstakingly made an animation using some much loved small felt mice. She had a big craze for a while for going to Royston market on a Saturday morning, where she bought cakes and jam from the WI stall, loving the domesticity and mocking the doilies in the same breath. Pop would take us to the epically good toyshop to look at Scalextric and model railways, but what I really loved doing, from then on, was raking through the bric-a-brac stalls. Lucy did too, and her funny kitsch taste for stuffed squirrels, square plates, souvenirs from the sort of seaside resorts she never went to and pressed glass coronation plates was unfamiliar and entertaining. Armed with these props and a very different taste in paint colours from Mum's, she made an ongoing trans-formation of the house which was both unsettling and also exciting.

Aged eight when I first met Lucy, and throughout my childhood, I was insufficiently confident to avoid a feeling that I had somehow to define and defend a slightly different predilection, expressed in worn copper lustreware, slightly-broken Staffordshire figures and little painted Victorian cream jugs. I think I loved these old-fashioned, chipped, gentle, flowery things a bit more fiercely because they were not quite in line with Lucy's tastes. The vast majority of the china on those market stalls in the late 1960s and 1970s was, to me at the time, almost invisible as I looked for survivors from earlier makers. The piles of TV-shaped plates, domino-spotted tea sets, tall thin coffee pots, and rioting turquoise and orange patterns everywhere were simply not interesting. But Lucy was good at picking amongst this stuff and putting it in surprising combinations on the now-repainted Bassingbourn kitchen dresser. She was also a winning cook; she made us apple fritters, and from her I learnt how to fillet a fish, joint a chicken and cook in a pressure cooker (a bit like driving a scary, miniature steam engine and it always impresses). Later on, as well as creating the great dressing-up box, she lent me her amazing clothes – and I mean, really amazing: an incredibly elegant white Edwardian suit; an almost-scandalous black sequinned dress; and lots of Ossie Clark. And she taught me how to pluck my eyebrows and shave my legs.

Lucy and Pop had two daughters together, Nancy and Daisy, and a bit later a son, Ben; while Mum and Rick had two daughters, Nell and Clover; so during my teens there were always small children to play with in both households, plus eggs to boil, prams to push, bathtimes for making soapy beards through the flannels. . . These two-sister partnerships (both pairs of my half-sisters, as well as the more distant example of Mum and her sister Teesa) became particularly clear and vitally interesting to me when Matthew and I left London in 1995, two years after Mum's accident. Our daughters, Elizabeth and Kitty, were five and three and already a powerful and admirable new version of this dynamic relationship. The move to a rented farmhouse in Worstead, very nearly in the Norfolk Broads, was made with the explicit plan of recovering our equilibrium after Mum's accident. Matthew and I set about making life really good fun, and it worked.

The girls wore fancy dress almost all the time, alternating bridesmaids' dresses and Princess Jasmine confections from Woolworths with ballet kit, which they quickly dumped when they saw what the girls wore for modern jazz after their ballet class in Stalham village hall – they lay on the floor and screamed for electric-blue leotards, and I admit that my resistance to the power of their combined plans was utterly futile: I gave in and bought the costumes. Mission accomplished, Lizzy and Kitty immediately lost interest in dance and wore the leotards non-stop, plus Barbie shoes. Just once in a while I weighed in and forced them into smocked linen dresses produced from Mum and Teesa's childhood by Granny, who lived nearby and seldom missed a picnic, and the two of them whizzed around the glorious acres of farm concrete (so handy for learning to ride a bike) like misplaced figures from a Caldecott fantasy of Edwardian childhood. They were inseparable, joined at the hip, partners with a complicity that fascinated me; they squared up to life and set about having fun with the most wonderful zest and unstoppable energy. In another context, Daisy declared of her closeness to Nancy that no one would ever manage to get so much as a cigarette paper between them, and I felt profound admiration, mixed with pride and some sadness, at this devout faith between sisters.

Picture the Rice family, still just four of us, in North Walsham in 1995. The unglamorous collection of shops there draws me, just like Royston used to draw Lucy, as an excellent place to trawl for props in a new life. Lizzy and Kitty, today wearing white tutus and pink gumboots, are developing an urgent need to own yet another small, caged creature and are having no difficulty in engaging Matthew in their schemes, which leaves me free to slope off and hunt for books, videos and serviceable blankets in the charity shops. That done I check on Matthew, who is now in the fish shop with the girls buying pints of brown shrimps, having promised them Woolworths next (as vital to them as Harrods was to his mum), so knowing they are happy, I can shop some more, focusing this time on the bric-a-brac shelves.

In the Break charity shop I find a very familiar abundance; here, all over again, are the TV-shaped plates, tall thin coffee pots, and turquoise and orange patterns. A sea change comes over me, a really dramatic moment of clear revelation, and I know that I love these things, all of them. For being unselfconscious and jolly, and for having been designed and made in Stoke. For being the end of the production line.

✳

Until the so-recent past we made unthinkably vast quantities of ware, not just for the home market but for half the world. The produce of the Potteries was shipped to all the corners of the British Empire, and beyond. Having developed this confidence, the makers boldly – perhaps even unthinkingly – expected to continue their dominance unchallenged. Wherever you go, you find evidence of this far-flung trade, from Willow pattern for homemakers out on the prairies of the American Midwest to spongeware in the souk in Damascus, and all manner of Staffordshire pottery in the markets in Africa, India and Sri Lanka. In Royston market in my childhood, the 'off the van' sales of loads of china told the story of struggle – the factories were achieving sales with increasing difficulty, indicating but not yet telling the dramatic changes sweeping towards them.

As late as 1965 there were still hundreds of factories all going full tilt, employing tens of thousands of people locally, but the wares I had ignored at the time were – I suddenly twigged – almost the last wave before the city was becalmed. And here in North Walsham the same wares were a poignant, silent army of witnesses, their backstamps a moving roll-call of the now empty, derelict or demolished factories that loomed so large in my imagination. Furnivals, Adderley, Baker, Midwinter, Ridgway, Masons, Beswick, Wade, Grindley, Carlton and lastly, but for Emma Bridgewater most significantly, Meakin. And this list names but a tiny handful – these businesses all gone now. And either the pigeons fly in and out of their broken windows now or more likely they are interred beneath a car park or supermarket.

Most tragically, their sites often stand empty, sometimes for years on end, as new developments are slow to gain steam; if only we could see the good sense of recycling these buildings and keeping their familiar shapes and encapsulated memories and culture! But not absolutely all of these old factories have fallen to the wrecking ball. The Meakin family operated their enormously successful business for about a century until they sold out to the Wedgwood Group in 1968. They mostly made tableware, in Hanley, in three big factories, one of which, called Eastwood Works, we bought in 1996. At that time it was dark, disused for several years and attracting the attention of vandals. We had a warehouse nearby for a while, so I was familiar with its long facade down Lichfield St and its broken windows. It is a copybook example of the type of derelict factory that I yearned to bring back to life when I first visited the city in 1984. Before the Clean Air

Act of 1956 there were seven splendid bottle kilns along the Caldon Canal, known affectionately as the Seven Sisters.

The pot banks closed in droves, and thousands of jobs were made redundant. Meanwhile similarly seismic changes were afflicting other heavy industries, and the local coal-mines and steelworks also closed. Like all the other cities of the Midlands, Stoke was plunged into long-term unemployment and the city has been wrestling valiantly ever since to work out how to reinvent itself. As diehard romantics, Matt and I cannot bear that the city should lose contact with its grand manufacturing past. Romance and nostalgia aside, I think that there is a clear strong case for evolving a new identity for the city using the powers of past traditions and achievements. I hope passionately that by specialising and by investing in design and marketing and modern management, the domestic china industry can flourish again. In the meantime the producers of robust ceramics for the hotel and catering trade have proved themselves more resilient businesses than most, and several of these are flourishing; along with a handful of other potteries, they are keeping the kilns firing.

✳

The china for sale today in every department store, kitchen, garden and gift shop is, almost without exception, made abroad. As such it is often pleasing and cheap, but it has not got a drop of the personality of the unfashionable and still slightly ungainly wares on the bric-a-brac shelves. The china offered now has no heart and soul, because it is not designed by one passionate person any longer. Instead it has been sourced by a buying team, whose mood board and brief indicate approximately to the faraway factory the ideas and colours they are to interpret. Whereas the square plates and tall coffee pots, and all the other cheerful Stoke-made things, were actually drawn: sometimes by a fancy, highly educated designer such as my mother-in-law, up from London, for sophisticated results; or, more often, by a local girl working in some badly-lit tucked-away part of the factory, dreaming of Spanish holidays or researching Mexican fiestas in the library. No matter how clumsy, the pieces had personality, provenance and real value. I started buying hungrily from the charity shops from that day on and – with Lucy's dresser in mind – I knew just how I would mix these orange and turquoise wares with Mum and Granny's gentler, older china. It turns out that what a pink lustre Victorian teapot cries out for is a pair of gold-rimmed plates decorated with images of Marilyn and Elvis.

Back in North Walsham in 1995, I buy half a pound of cheese straws from the baker and go to find Matthew and the girls.

WHAT IS IT ABOUT
KITCHEN DRESSERS?

IT IS POSSIBLE that I am more aware of what is on my kitchen dresser than I am of the contents of my wardrobe. It's also likely that I have spent more, over the years, on dressing my dresser than on dressing myself. If that's an exaggeration, I have certainly spent more on china than I have on shoes. . . And I have to work at it to get excited about clothes, whereas I'm always up for a fancy early-nineteenth-century coffee jug, or a mid-twentieth-century one for that matter; maybe it's because you don't have to go through the wearisome business of trying them on. Alone and wrestling into the wrong jeans in an undersized cubicle, or wishing myself anywhere but the communal changing rooms of Miss Selfridge, where

I vividly remember Mum and my headmistress chatting unconcernedly as they swapped party dresses and stood around in their underwear – I always feel defeated before I start. Whereas filling a battered cardboard box with eighteen green spongeware cups and saucers (plus four more cups bearing the legend Marsh Lane Chapel added as an irresistible afterthought), all tenderly wrapped in newspaper – this is an endless pleasure and I always want more.

It seems that I am not unusual in my passionate attachment to the pottery that Matthew and I have collected together. I have had so many extraordinary conversations with people – women usually, although I do have some remarkable and dedicated male collectors as well, I'm very happy to say – about the fact that our favourite china is with us through all the good times and the bad, always there, always comforting, familiar and speaking of home, silent witness to triumph and disaster, as well as all the everyday stuff which makes up our lives.

Our collectors are a doughty and marvellous bunch, who form friend groups at our collector events, meet up on Facebook, and swap and squirrel enormous quantities of pottery, following the form on eBay, eagle-eyed for rising interest in discontinued patterns. They enter all our schemes for flower shows, cake stalls and team lunches.

They have even been known to camp out in Stoke to ensure first place in the queue at our sales. But above all, they each and every one confirm my theory that kitchen china really matters to us because it's a renewable means by which to manifest our ideas of home, friendships and family, and the ways in which we sustain each other by offering warmth and welcome.

Someone once suggested to me that, for the urban housewife with only a backyard or a window box in which to express herself horticulturally, maybe arranging a dresser full of flowery china was 'displaced gardening', akin to training a wisteria or tying up a climbing rose and a clematis on the same wall. This picturesque image has stayed in my mind, I think because until that moment I had not asked myself the question: *What is going on when I arrange china on a dresser?* I'd simply taken it for granted as one of the hundreds of jobs that go on in any household, albeit one of the nicest. It is in the same category as choosing a selection of nice pillowcases when making up a bed; or dyeing all the tired-looking bath towels deep pink; or polishing the battered assortment of silver plate cutlery; or washing, scraping and polishing the forest of wax-encrusted brass candlesticks we use on the kitchen table. Other homemaking tasks in the same vein include making marmalade, or jam, or jelly, and then labelling it nicely; and polishing up a brass fish kettle and filling it with pink hyacinth bulbs to stow in a cupboard, ready to flower at Christmas. These are the sort of small-scale, slightly fiddly projects which define 'home'. They all say a lot about you and your house, as well as being soothing and pleasing – but as I consider the matter, I am sure that getting the dresser right is the central thing for me.

∗

If you are lucky, you might find a house with a big capacious dresser already built in, designed to (most likely) Edwardian standards of kitchen equipment, like the pitch pine dresser in the kitchen at Bassingbourn, in what had been the farmhouse of a big busy farm, which called for a large dinner service. The telephone (with the first number I can remember – easy, as it was just three digits; you rang the operator to call outside the exchange) sat at one end. The pretty dinner service on it wasn't what we used every day, so the look of that particular dresser didn't change much. Tom and I climbed up on the telephone chair periodically to look into a white china hen on a nest (Portmeirion, I'm pretty sure) into which Mum emptied a box of Smarties sometimes. And we made camps in the cupboards, displacing the Christmas decorations.

When Mum moved to Oxford, the house she bought was large and dilapidated, with a chipped and battered dresser built in, filling one whole wall in the kitchen. As with the rest of the house in Rawlinson Road, she did not bother to repaint it, instead covering it with a patchwork of china, old and new, having left her wedding china (which was Wedgwood Figs) behind in Bassingbourn. She applied a similar approach to the shabby kitchen walls, making a collage of our paintings, posters and magazine cuttings, all unframed and sometimes graffiti'd. The dresser did not just hold china, but also letters, cards or invitations that she especially loved, and a comic china cat with fetching ringlets and a lacy décolletage, as well as desiccated bridesmaid's bouquets, keys, and a row of paperbacks. We wrote telephone numbers on the wall beside the dresser, and ever since I have liked the look of writing on the wall. It is such a tempting thing to see that clean blank space. When Lizzy was a teenager, she and her friends took this to an extreme, using her bedroom walls as a giant notice board, scrawled with messages, lyrics and phone numbers.

The central pieces, on the high and wide shelves, is where I start when I am rearranging my dresser, which I have to do much more often than I would in a perfect world, due to the large number of photographic shoots from our catalogues which happen in our kitchen. I arrange meat plates, cake plates and serving pieces which would usually only come down from time to time to play their parts at parties, for big cuts of meat, or for birthday cakes or towers of choux buns ready to have chocolate sauce poured all over them. Then I add decorative plates, balancing the mismatched patterns on either side of the central heroes. The smaller things follow last, always finding the spot where they can talk to the other patterns around them. I'm reminded of places, parties and people as I juggle the familiar pieces into pleasing groups.

I think that Mum was using the dresser in the kitchen in Oxford as a giant collage illustrating family life. Each and every thing on it was something of specific value and significance, and arranging them so that they made a pleasing picture was a way of making a statement of her style, and our life. She declared on her dresser that matching sets were redundant, that you should follow your heart, and that if you did, you would make harmony out of dissonance. She rewrote the script for her family life, illustrating that we could all get on, that broken things can be mended or put to a different use, and that this is a process of daily slight readjustment. She would think that to say this is to overstate it, and by now she would be yawning rather impatiently, and I would stop myself abruptly and suggest making a pot of tea in her pewter teapot. And she would be pleased, especially if there was ginger cake to go with it.

GINGER CAKE
WITH MARMALADE

✳ ✳ ✳

This ginger cake recipe is delicious on its own; it was given to Mum by Desmond's sister Mary MacCarthy. The marmalade addition was my idea.

Grease and line a 20cm deep, round, loose-bottomed cake tin or spring-form tin with non-stick baking paper and spread the base with 5–6 table-spoons of dark, thick-cut marmalade. Warm 150ml milk, 100g butter, 100g moist sugar (soft light brown or light muscovado) and 225g black treacle together in a saucepan. Add 225g plain flour, 1 teaspoon of ground ginger and ¼ teaspoon of bicarbonate of soda. Mix together and then add 2 medium eggs and beat well. Put into the tin and bake in a moderate oven set at 170°C/150°C fan/gas 3 for approximately 55 minutes until a skewer comes away cleanly.

ACKNOWLEDGEMENTS

* * *

Inevitably these stories only introduce you to a tiny number of the huge crowds of people to whom the company owes its existence, and I so many bushels of bouquets and gratitude. To be clear, I have not included again here those named elsewhere in the book; and many others than those listed between these covers have played roles great and small. It would fill too many pages if I were to list each and every name, but please understand from the following (incomplete!) roll call that my career has truly, at every step, been a team event. I begin with an apology for an interminably long Oscars-speech-type roll call, but that's the way it is. All of these people played their parts and without them there would be no EB. . .

Dick Sale ran first the factory, then the company, with characteristic energy and thoughtfulness. Judy Shawcross knew everything, about everyone, and checked me when I went too far. Jamie, her wonderful son, ran the shops and so much more that we feared we would fall to bits when he left. Julie Cockburn made light of so many tedious trade fairs; she even made me look forward to them. Kelvin New saved the company more than once and persuaded me to grow up – all whilst either out hunting, or racing his beautiful classic cars. Antonia Williams was my very first assistant and I still miss her; Fiona Milne was my first proper customer and she inspired me to live up to her faith in the company; William Kendall pulled us out of the dark ages; Geoff Handcock showed me how to start growing up in business; and James Benfield continued these difficult lessons with good humour. Johnny Jourdan was as fierce as if he were my (handsome, bearded) older brother through my factory dramas; Marion has been a true friend from the early years. Thank you Sue Appleton, Sue Chapman and Sue O'Brien: sisters, all.

Lucy Catling is a miracle: her energy, attention to detail and unfailing sweet temper make life every day more effective and much nicer. Gail, I still miss every day. Marion has been an unfailing friend and help through so many regime changes, along with all the kind and efficient people in the Stoke office! Leigh is Potteries royalty, and we are privileged to have her heading up our studio in the factory, along with wonderful Will, tall and helpful Ashley, amazing Rachel, and lovely, deft-fingered Lynsey. Mark Thomas has been a tower of strength; his production expertise offset my ignorance and he has a tireless team – thank you lovely Janice, Steve, Carol, Nigel, Angela, Alan, Julie and Andy. Our warehouse regularly performs miracles – thank you to all of you, but especially Nicky. Our shops are friendly and efficient because of Zoe, Anusia, Christina, Henrietta and Minerva. And the nerve centre – the Fulham office – has been powered by Matt Dobson, calmed and focused by Julia, energised by beautiful Dana, decorated by Sarah DB and made sense of by Katy, whilst Victoria has been an inspiration. (And so many teatime meetings have been immeasurably improved by Caryl's biscuits.)

Thank you to each and every one of the men and women who work in the different workshops of our factory: you are the salt of the earth and the bearers of a long tradition. I am privileged to work with you.

How can it be possible that none of these people feature in the book – or only as walk-ons? I can only say lamely that I have not set out to be comprehensive, but instead to try to convey an impression of how it felt, and how a small representative group of friends and family, colleagues and contemporaries – as well as a ghostly host of designers, writers, even singers, many dead – have all played a part in forming me, the company and its products.

In the making of this book I have been bowled over by the calm of my wise editor Elizabeth Hallett; and I am indebted to Sarah Ballard, my agent, for her persistence in writing to me annually for a lot of years, gently persuading me to start telling this story. Thank you to Ami Smithson for her patience and inspiration, and to Kate Miles, and to Bryony Nowell for painstakingly checking my many inaccuracies. If any errors have slipped through, they are entirely my fault and no one else's!

I have been lucky to be part of a huge and variegated family, all of whom have been supporters from the start; these are my wonderful siblings: Sophy, Tom, Nancy, Daisy, Nell, Clover and Ben.

But most of all thank you forever to Elizabeth, Kitty, Margaret and Michael: you have had to sit through interminable conversations during innumerable car journeys, hearing about everything from factory productivity, design management, waste management and website development, to the details of meetings and partings. You must so often have longed for me to join an order of Trappist nuns – please forgive me!

In writing these stories, I mined the past to find motives and inspirations that lay in my childhood, and also in the very early days of the first beginnings of the company, in 1984. Just three years after that I met Matthew, and the plain truth is that since then, through thick and thin, he has been my North Star. We have worked together, often at the same desk, and to him I owe the greatest debt of all, and that feels really nice.